Our Lady of the Atonement
Catholic Church
San Antonio, Texas

Inquiry Class

Study Questions
and
Supplemental Materials

Sixth Edition
Copyright June 2022
All Rights Reserved

Table of Cont<barcode MW01107465>

INTRODUCTION

READING ASSIGNMENTS

All reading assignments are from the *Compendium: Catechism of the Catholic Church (CCCC)*. The page numbers in the CCCC and the relevant question numbers are provided. Please read each of these assignments prior to that session.

ABOUT THE STUDY QUESTIONS

The Gospel demands a response from us. It is critical to think about the implications of what you are studying for your daily life. We must first understand what God offers us and then evaluate our response to God's offer, to include how we live our lives. While reading the assignments consider the questions which are designed to help you learn and remember the key concepts of each session. After attending each lecture, go back, review the relevant questions, your lecture notes, and any handouts and write out what you understand. We have placed in parentheses relevant question numbers from the *Compendium: Catechism of the Catholic Church (CCCC)*. Let us know if we can help clarify any of these questions or any of your later follow-on questions.

ABOUT THE SUPPLEMENTAL MATERIALS

The supplemental materials began as handouts for each session. Managing the large number of handouts became difficult, especially with multiple handouts for some sessions. Students did not always have the handouts with them when needed for succeeding classes making it difficult to refer back to previous handouts. Having all of the supplemental handouts in one volume makes it easier to ensure that everyone receives all handouts, we have enough copies for everyone, and handouts are always available to the student. Please bring this book with you to every class.

OTHER REFERENCES

The current Inquiry Class schedule is displayed at Our Lady of the Atonement's web site at www.ourladyoftheatonement.org, select "Learn," then select "Adult Inquiry Class."

BIBLE TRANSLATIONS

There are many English translations of the Bible, some of which are Catholic. A good Catholic translation of the Bible is important to have. Following are short descriptions of some Catholic translations.

New American Bible (NAB): this is approved by the United States Conference of Catholic Bishops (USCCB) for general liturgical use in the United States. There are many editions of this translation, the latest came out in 2000-2002. This latest edition is the most reliable and is the version used in the liturgy in most dioceses of the United States. Earlier editions were generally much less reliable translations. Unfortunately, the commentary at the bottom of each page included in many publishers' versions of the NAB is not always reliable and should generally be disregarded.

Revised Standard Version-Catholic Edition (RSV-CE): This is a very good translation and is usually one of the best version for Bible studies. It is approved for use in the United States and is the translation used for Mass at Our Lady of the Atonement. There is a New Revised Standard (NRSV) edition which is not approved for use in the liturgy because of its inappropriate and misleading use of so-called inclusive language. For this reason, the NRSV is not generally recommended. There is also a second version of the RSV-CE which is called the RSV-2CE. The RSV-2CE version primarily eliminates the older terminology (Thee, Thou, hast, etc.). We do not use this version in the liturgy at Our Lady of the Atonement, but it is also good for Bible studies.

English Standard Version-Catholic Edition (ESV-CE): There is also another Catholic translation which begins with the RSV, but it is a major revision of the RSV. While it shared with the RSV-2CE the primary emphasis of removing the same older terminology, it also went through most the Bible's books to reflect the latest in terms of research in establishing the best estimate for the original text (called the critical edition). Like the RSV-CE and RSV-2CE this translation is good for Bible studies.

Jerusalem Bible (JB): This translation is also approved for the Mass in the United States. It maintains some older English and is also a good translation for Bible studies. There is also a New Jerusalem Bible (NJB) which, like the NRSV, is not approved for use in the Mass for the same reason and should likewise be avoided.

Douai-Rheims (DR): This translation was made in the late 16th century in France for use in England during the penal times during which Catholics were prohibited from practicing their faith. It uses archaic English and was used as the English translation for the liturgy until the NAB. For communities using the Extraordinary Form of the liturgy (the Mass said in Latin using the approved Roman Missal of 1962), the English translations of the Latin provided in liturgical aids still use parts of this translation.

Confraternity Edition (CE): This translation was begun in the 1930s but was never completed. The parts of the Bible for which the English translations were completed were substituted for the DR in the translation aids of the Latin used during the liturgy. It is also still found in these aides used in the Extraordinary Form of the liturgy said today.

SESSION 1: TRUTH, AUTHORITY, FAITH AND THE CREED

READING ASSIGNMENT

Pages 1-6: questions 1-5; pages 11-19: questions 25-44; pages 192-193

STUDY QUESTIONS

Truth:

- What is truth? (Consider CCCC questions (qq): 41, 87)
- Can we actually know the truth? (CCCC qq: 3, 4, 5, 18)
- Why is the truth important? (CCCC qq: 1, 2, 6, 25, 521, 526)

Authority:

- What is authority? (CCCC qq: 39, 52)
- Is submitting to authority in matters of faith reasonable? (CCCC qq: 4, 11, 15, 16, 17)
- Is submitting to authority contrary to human dignity? (CCCC qq: 363, 364)

Faith:

- What is faith? (CCCC qq: 27, 28)
- How does one come to faith (personal and communal)? (CCCC qq: 30, 32)
- Why is faith required for salvation? (CCCC qq: 27, 366)

The Apostles and Nicene Creed:

- What does the Creed indicate about the corporate nature of man's relationship with God? (CCCC qq: 33, 36, 39, 40, 42)
- What does the Creed indicate about the need for adherence to truth for authentic unity? (CCCC qq: 41, 42)
- What does the Holy Spirit as the source of unity and communion show about our communion with God and one another? (CCCC qq: 138, 143, 144, 145, 146)

NOTES:

WHY IT'S IMPORTANT TO ASK FUNDAMENTAL QUESTIONS

We are made for more

God calls us to communion with Him. Communion is what we are ultimately made for. This is what St. Augustine meant when he said, "our hearts are restless until they find rest in Thee O Lord." If we reflect upon our experiences, we can find numerous instances in our lives in which we obtain some sought after goal and ultimately are left unsatisfied. This happens in the acquisition of things, in attaining important accomplishments, in developing personal relationships, etc. Our inability to be ultimately satisfied by any created thing points us to our need for some final completion, some final fulfilment. Our ultimate fulfillment can only be obtained from a proper relationship with God.

Among all the things we attain, we can easily see that the most satisfying are our relationships with others. This is because we are also made for communion with others. Communion is the key. It is defined as a relationship of selfless love. What this tells us, and which we can verify through our experiences, is that the more selfless we are in our relationships the more satisfying they are. Selflessness does not mean allowing others to misuse and abuse us; nor does it mean giving others everything they want. This is not selflessness. Selflessness is willing and acting in a way that is for the authentic good of the other person, regardless of self-interest. The good of the other person doesn't mean allowing one to act in a selfish or harmful manner. Authentic selflessness is found in helping each person to achieve holiness, regardless of self-interest.

Our communion with others is the most personally satisfying because personal relationships of selfless love is what we are made for. In the next few weeks of our Inquiry Class sessions, we will look at why this is and why communion with God requires first God's gift of Himself to us and then our response to His gifts. We will also discuss this call to communion with God in terms of how and why He calls us, problems that have arisen in human history preventing communion with Him, and what God has done in order to overcome these problems. This in a nutshell summarizes the entirety of the Christian faith. However, we first ought to look at some issues that make it hard for us in today's society to hear and accept God's call to communion.

Belief and Trust in a skeptical world

Belief in ultimate things, God and heaven, is not a mundane question such as "will I choose one profession or another?". The choice to believe in God and to accept His offer of everlasting life is the most fundamental question for each and every human person. Belief is the response to an essential demand upon the human person to act or to refuse to act in accord with his nature. For this reason, the fundamental questions, "who am I?," "why do I exist?, what is ultimately real?" can be ignored only to our peril.

The requirement to believe is not unreasonable. In fact, belief corresponds to human nature. We are made to believe because we are made for relationships with God and others. Belief is necessary for any authentic, reciprocal relationship of love. The prerequisite to belief is trust and so trust is also a requirement for personal fulfillment because our fulfillment is found only and ultimately in a relationship of love with God.

We can see from our experiences that it is in fact reasonable and necessary to trust in daily life because our daily life is permitted only through relationships of trust with others, most of whom we do not personally know. We trust in order to learn. In fact, we do not learn unless we first develop trust with the one who teaches us. Those who tabulate such things estimate that more than 90% of what we think we know we have been taught by others by trusting them and what they have told us. Children learn by first trusting their parents and they completely trust until they learn that they cannot trust. We say that they lose their innocence when they learn that not all people can always be trusted.

Those who do not learn the virtue of prudence, which is to determine when to withhold trust, we call naïve. Our experience reveals that trust in others is most natural to us and it is also necessary if we are to live healthily and fruitfully. Distrust is not in accord with human nature. In fact, distrust is a direct result of original sin.

Societies require trust to function because they are a web of relationships. We must first trust if we are to live and thrive in society. We can easily see this is what we normally do. Stepping out the door in the morning requires trust that the first person you meet will not try to harm you. Driving on the road requires we generally trust people to obey the traffic laws and not actively try to hit us. Buying groceries from the store first requires trust that the food is safe to eat. Getting to know a person requires that you trust what they say when they tell you about themselves

Prudence versus Skepticism

While love is first a matter of choosing, an intimate relationship of selfless love requires trust. These relationships of selfless love are necessary for man's fulfillment because we are made in the image of God, a God Who is Love itself. Man requires love, to love and to be loved, in order to flourish, in order to be fulfilled. It follows then, that trust is fundamental to the meaning of the human person. The corollary to this truth then is that habitual skepticism is destructive to the human person.

However, this is not to say that prudence is not needed. We live in a state of the fall; that is, our natural experiences are combined with "unnatural" consequences of original sin. This means that not everyone is always trustworthy. We often violate the natural order (e.g., we are not always truthful). There are circumstances in which we need to exhibit prudential caution. But prudential caution is not the same as suspicion. Being prudentially cautious is recognizing that at certain times one must be more careful before acting. For example, when the consequences are grave (e.g., the safety of a child) and/or the risk is sufficiently high (e.g., we are dealing with someone who has been habitually untruthful in similar circumstances) that there will be negative consequences in trusting someone.

Even if some suggest that it is best to be skeptical, no one can live being consistently skeptical. Such an attitude is destructive for relationships and damaging to the human person. In reality, those who advocate suspicion or skepticism usually reserve their skepticism for just a few areas. Usually, those areas are where they have been hurt or in which the demands on their life are higher than they are willing to accept. Succumbing to skepticism is ultimately rejection of who we are and what we are made for. Skepticism makes our human relationships difficult, and it undermines our ability to hear and to respond to God.

Man as Seeker of Truth

Man is made to seek the truth. Within his very being, he cannot be satisfied if he is not convinced he rests in the truth. This need to seek and possess the truth is the drive behind man's insatiable curiosity and his desire to know. Nevertheless, it is true that some individuals can develop bad habits through negative experiences or making a habit of lazy living to suppress this natural desire to seek and know truth. Therefore, to live in accord with the way we were made, we must pursue the truth.

It is true that everyone naturally pursues truth (or at least must convince themselves they are seeking the truth). This can be demonstrated most clearly among those who fall into the error of theoretical relativism. Even such a person intuitively realizes that there is ultimate truth and that it is possible to find it or he would not be seeking it. It is ironic that this ultimate truth the relativist believes he has found is that there is no ultimate truth. But this is self-contradictory. It is not possible for anyone who is not all-knowing to suppose he can rule out all truth. He admits that there is ultimate truth by claiming to know the truth, while at the same time denying it. We have been given an intellect to be able to pursue and to know when we have found truth.

Faith and Reason

We live in a society that thankfully acknowledges the achievements of modern science, but all too often we are falsely led to believe that modern science is the only reliable source of truth. This error is called "scientism", which is assuming that if a claim does not come from the methods of science than it is simply opinion. An even more erroneous assumption of scientism is that an assertion from someone who has some sort of credibility as a scientist cannot be argued with, often regardless of the topic, while assertions by others are simply opinions. What underlies the error of scientism is the assumption that modern science is the only source of real knowledge, that is, all real knowledge can be subject to the demand of "prove it."

Not all knowledge falls into this category. In fact, not all scientific claims can be proven (or falsified). Ironically, the kind of knowledge that can be proven by what we call the scientific method is actually the least certain of the kinds of knowledge that we have. The reason for this is modern science is empirical, it is knowledge based upon our observation of instances of things (in Greek, *emperia*). For most knowledge, we will never be able to observe all possible events, all circumstances, or all instances of anything. This means that such knowledge is always open to revision as we learn more. However, there are two other types of knowledge that do not require the observation of instances of things and so they are more certain.

There is knowledge that comes to us simply by reflecting upon the world that we can see reflectively. The most certain knowledge we can have by reason alone is that which we cannot prove (though we can demonstrate to be necessary). This knowledge comes under the category of first philosophical principles. For example, first principles of thinking cannot be proved or they would not be first principles. But without such first principles, we could never get started thinking because we would forever have to regress to an earlier principle to prove the one we wish to start from. One of the most important of these first principles of thought is the law of non-contradiction which says something cannot both be and not be at the same time and in the same way. We all assume this principle to be true and depend upon it. Modern science would be impossible without it (indeed, thinking itself would be impossible). But because modern science is limited to empirical methods it leaves scientists with nothing to say about philosophical first principles except to presuppose their truth.

The knowledge with the most certainty of truth is divine revelation, because it comes from God who cannot deceive or be deceived. God, who is omnipotent cannot be limited by man's limitations. It is not reasonable to point to man's limitedness as preventing God from revealing himself without error to His Church. However, access to this knowledge requires a more explicit encounter with faith. More explicit because as we already indicated, faith and trust in others is fundamental to being human and is something we do almost without thinking.

Faith is not something that can be proved or else it is not faith. But while it cannot be proved in the mathematical sense, it can be shown to be reasonable. In fact, to be believable the first prerequisite is that it is reasonable, meaning that any authentic doctrine cannot be a real contradiction. Faith is reasonable but faith is not the same as reason. While authentic Christian doctrines are always reasonable, they oftentimes require us to go beyond merely human reason (but never against it).

Faith has two interrelated but distinct aspects. First, faith is an act of the will that begins with trust and second, faith is our acceptance of and commitment to someone's revelation about himself. Faith is the full commitment of one person to a relationship of trust with another person. However, this relationship must also be based upon a knowledge of the person. This is true of human relationships and certainly true of our relationship with God. Religious faith is a complete commitment to a relationship of love with God. This is essentially our response to His invitation, because He loves us first. This relationship is based upon our desire to know and accept God's revelation to us about Himself. In other words, in committing to Christ we are committing to Him as He has revealed Himself in the entire content of the Catholic faith.

One other aspect of faith in God is supernatural. God responds to our commitment to believe with a supernatural gift of Himself which we call "grace". This grace supernaturally strengthens our human act of faith in Him and His revelation beyond that which is possible through human reason alone.

EARLY CHURCH TESTIMONY ON CONTINUING APOSTOLIC AUTHORITY

"The Apostles received the gospel for us from the Lord Jesus Christ; and Jesus Christ was sent from God. Christ, therefore, is from God, and the Apostles are from Christ. Both of these orderly arrangements, then, are by God's will. ...Through the countryside and city they preached; and they appointed their earliest converts, testing them by the spirit, to be the bishops and deacons of future believers. Nor was this a novelty, for bishops and deacons had been written about a long time earlier. ...Our apostles knew through our Lord Jesus Christ that there would be strife for the office of bishop. For this reason, therefore, having received perfect foreknowledge, they appointed those who have already been mentioned and afterwards added the further provision that, if they should die, other approved men should succeed to their ministry"

St. Clement of Rome, *Letter to the Corinthians* (AD 80)

"You must follow the bishop as Jesus Christ follows the Father, and the presbytery as you would the Apostles. ...Let no one do anything of concern to the Church without the bishop... Wherever the bishop appears, let the people be there; just as wherever Jesus Christ is, there is the Catholic Church."

St. Ignatius of Antioch, *Letter to the Smyrnaeans* (AD 107)

"In like manner let everyone respect the deacons as they would respect Jesus Christ, and just as they respect the bishop as a type of the Father, and the presbyters as the council of God and college of Apostles. Without these, it cannot be called a Church."

St. Ignatius of Antioch, *Letter to the Trallians* (AD 110)

"It is possible, then, for everyone in every Church, who may wish to know the truth, to contemplate the tradition of the Apostles which has been made known throughout the whole world. And we are in a position to enumerate those who were instituted bishops by the Apostles, and their successors to our own times: ... The blessed Apostles [Peter and Paul], having founded and built up the Church [of Rome], they handed over the office of the episcopate to Linus. Paul makes mention of this Linus in the Epistle to Timothy. To him succeeded Anencletus; and after him, in the third place from the Apostles, Clement was chosen for the episcopate. He had seen the blessed Apostles and was acquainted with them. ...To this Clement, Evaristus succeeded; and Alexander succeeded Evaristus. Then, sixth after the Apostles, Sixtus was appointed; after him, Telesphorus, who also was gloriously martyred. ... In the order, and by the teaching of the Apostles handed down in the Church, the preaching of the truth has come down to us."

St. Irenaeus, *Against Heresies* (AD 180)

"When I had come to Rome, I [visited] Anicetus, whose deacon was Eleutherus. And after Anicetus [died], Soter succeeded, and after him Eleutherus. In each succession and in each city there is a continuance of that which is proclaimed by the law, the prophets, and the Lord"

Hegesippus, *Memoirs* (cited in Eusebius, *Ecclesiastical History*) (AD 180)

"There is one God, and one Christ, and one Church, and one Chair founded on Peter by the word of the Lord. It is not possible to set up another altar or for there to be another priesthood besides that one altar and the one priesthood. Whoever has gathered elsewhere is scattering."

St. Cyprian of Carthage, *Letter to all his People* (AD 251)

"With a false bishop appointed for themselves by heretics, they dare even to set sail and carry letters from schismatics and blasphemers to the chair of Peter and to the principal Church, in which sacerdotal unity has its source; nor did they take thought that these are Romans, whose faith was praised by the preaching Apostle, and among whom it is not possible for perfidy to have entrance."

St. Cyprian of Carthage, *Letter to Cornelius* (AD 252)

"Far be it from me to speak adversely of any of these clergy who, in succession from the apostles, confect by their sacred word the Body of Christ and through whose efforts also it is that we are Christians."

St. Jerome, *Letters* (AD 396)

"[T]here are many other things which most properly can keep me in [the Catholic Church's] bosom. The unanimity of peoples and nations keeps me here. Her authority, inaugurated in miracles, nourished by hope, augmented by love, and confirmed by her age, keeps me here. The succession of priests, from the very see of the apostle Peter, to whom the Lord, after his resurrection, gave the charge of feeding his sheep [John 21:15–17], up to the present episcopate, keeps me here. And last, the very name Catholic, which, not without reason, belongs to this Church alone, in the face of so many heretics, so much so that, although all heretics want to be called 'Catholic,' when a stranger inquires where the Catholic Church meets, none of the heretics would dare to point out his own basilica or house."

St. Augustine, *Against the Letter of Mani Called "The Foundation"* (AD 397)

The Apostles' Creed

1 I believe in God, the Father almighty, Creator of heaven and earth,

2 and in Jesus Christ, His only Son, our Lord,

3 who was conceived by the Holy Spirit, born of the Virgin Mary,

4 suffered under Pontius Pilate, was crucified, died, and was buried.

5 He descended into hell; on the third day he rose again from the dead.

6 He ascended into heaven and sits at the right hand of God the Father almighty,

7 From thence He shall come to judge the living and the dead.

8 I believe in the Holy Spirit,

9 the Holy Catholic Church, the communion of saints,

10 the forgiveness of sins,

11 the resurrection of the body,

12 and life everlasting. Amen.

The Nicene Creed

International Commission on English in the Liturgy (ICEL)

I believe in one God, the Father Almighty, maker of heaven and earth, of all things visible and invisible.

I believe in one Lord, Jesus Christ, the only begotten Son of God, born of the Father before all ages. God from God, Light from Light, true God from true God, begotten, not made, consubstantial with the Father; through him all things were made.

For us men and for our salvation he came down from heaven,
(bow in honor of the Incarnation; genuflect at Christmas and on the Feast of the Annunciation) and by the Holy Spirit was incarnate of the Virgin Mary, and became man. *(stand)*

For our sake he was crucified under Pontius Pilate, he suffered death and was buried, and rose again on the third day in accordance with the Scriptures.

He ascended into heaven and is seated at the right hand of the Father.

He will come again in glory to judge the living and the dead and his kingdom will have no end.

I believe in the Holy Spirit, the Lord, the giver of life, who proceeds from the Father and the Son; who with the Father and the Son is adored and glorified, who has spoken through the prophets.

I believe in one, holy, catholic and apostolic Church. I confess one Baptism for the forgiveness of sins; and I look forward to the resurrection of the dead and the life of the world to come.   Amen.

Nicene Creed as said in the "Anglican Use"

I believe in one God, the Father Almighty, maker of heaven and earth, and of all things visible and invisible.

And in one Lord, Jesus Christ, the only begotten Son of God, begotten of His Father before all worlds. God of God, Light of Light, very God of very God, begotten, not made, being of one substance with the Father; by whom all things were made; who for us men and for our salvation, came down from heaven,
(genuflect in honor of the Incarnation) and was incarnate by the Holy Ghost of the Virgin Mary, and was made man; *(stand)* and was crucified also for us under Pontius Pilate; he suffered and was buried; and the third day He rose again according to the Scriptures, and ascended into heaven, and sitteth on the right hand of the Father; and He shall come again, with glory, to judge both the quick and the dead; whose kingdom will have no end.

And I believe in the Holy Ghost the Lord, and Giver of life, who proceedeth from the Father and the Son; and with the Father and the Son together is worshipped and glorified; who spake by the prophets.

And I believe one, holy, catholic and Apostolic Church. I acknowledge one Baptism for the remission of sins; and I look for to the resurrection of the dead, and the life of the world to come.
Amen.

APOSTLES CREED: The Apostles Creed is the ancient baptismal Creed used by the Church in Rome for those in the first centuries of the Church who received Baptism at the Easter Vigil. In a slightly different form, it was known as the "Old Roman Creed" during these early centuries. It is considered "the oldest Roman Catechism" (CCC 196). The Church has always considered this Creed to be of great authority because it constituted the Church of Rome's faithful preservation of the tradition handed on by the Apostles. We have this testimony from the great 4th century Bishop of Milan, St. Ambrose: "[it is] the Creed of the Roman Church, the See of Peter, the first of the apostles, to which he brought the common faith" (Sermon 38).

There is a later apocryphal tradition that says each of the twelve Apostles contributed an article of faith to the Creed. While this is not likely, the tradition has long been maintained in the form of the Apostles' Creed division into twelve articles. The *Catechism of the Catholic Church* uses this twelve-article structure for the first of its four pillars (for more on the *Catechism* see page 33).

NICENE CREED (or more precisely the Niceno-Constantinopolitan Creed): Throughout the life of the Church, previously unasked questions about the faith are always arising. At times theologians make missteps in trying to answer them, but most allow themselves to be corrected by the Church's Magisterium (i.e., the Church's teaching office comprised of the bishops in communion with the pope). Sometimes those making errors refuse correction; at other times, even a bishop can make an error. In the early Church, if an error became too disruptive to the life of the local church and it could not be resolved by the local bishop, regional bishops would gather together to address the matter in what was called a synod (if it involved the universal Church under the authority of the pope it was called an ecumenical council). At times, the result of the local synod was an addition to a local creed in order to proclaim the true faith and to correct the error that had been causing confusion. Modifications to the universal Creed happened only twice in ecumenical councils; at the Council of Nicaea in AD 325 and at the Council of Constantinople in AD 381.

Some of the most perplexing questions for the early Church concerned understanding the doctrine of the Trinity and the Incarnation. A Libyan priest named Arius tried to resolve the question of the nature of the Son of God, falsely teaching that He was a creature, but the highest of all creatures, because he couldn't see how there could be only one God if the Son were also God. Arius would not allow himself to be corrected by his bishop and was so effective in promoting his erroneous teaching that the entire Roman Empire became embroiled in the controversy. So much so, that with the agreement of the pope, Emperor Constantine called for a council to be held at Nicaea. The result of this ecumenical council was that the Creed was modified to correct Arius's error, proclaiming the Apostolic Faith that the Son is of the same nature (i.e., God) as the Father, using the term "consubstantial." Additional questions subsequently arose which also became sufficiently contentious that the bishops met again in 381 at Constantinople, clarifying that the Holy Spirit is also God and correcting other errors. The Creed from Constantinople is the form that has been said in the Church ever since with the exception that at the beginning of the second millennium, the entire Latin Church adopted the Synod of Toledo's (AD 589) modification to the Creed to add the clarification "and the Son" (*Filioque*) after the phrase "Who proceeds from the Father." Because the modifications at Constantinople were so considerable, the formal name of the Creed we profess today is the Niceno-Constantinopolitan Creed, but it is often shortened to the Nicene Creed. Because it is said during Mass as the summary of our Christian faith, it is also referred to as the Profession of Faith.

NOTES

SESSION 2: DIVINE REVELATION & INTRODUCTION TO SCRIPTURE

READING ASSIGNMENT

Pages 5-10: questions 1-24

STUDY QUESTIONS

Divine Revelation:

- What is Divine Revelation? (CCCC qq: 7, 8, 9, 12, 14)
- How does one know where to find it? (CCCC qq: 11, 13, 15, 20)
- How does one know its authentic meaning? (CCCC qq: 16, 17, 18, 19, 21, 22)

Tradition:

- What is the relationship between Tradition and Scripture? (CCCC q: 17)
- What do we mean by Tradition? (CCCC qq: 11-17)

Scripture:

- What do we mean by divine inspiration and the inerrancy of Scripture? (CCCC q: 18)
- How are we to read Scripture? (CCCC q: 19)

NOTES:

A Tutorial on Sacred Scripture

Divine Revelation: God reveals Himself to us through His Son, the Eternal Word of the Father. The name "Word" reveals to us that all we can know of God is known through His Son. When we think of the Word, therefore, we should first think about a Divine Person rather than primarily His works and life written down in Sacred Scripture. The Son revealed Himself, through the power of the Holy Spirit, gradually over many millennia, through words and deeds among His people. God spoke in various ways (including visions and dreams) until the time He enters history in a most surprising way (see Hebrews 1:1-2 [this reference refers to the Letter to the Hebrews in the New Testament, chapter 1, verses 1 through 2]). The fullness of Revelation comes to man when the Word takes upon Himself, Flesh. God is now fully revealed in Jesus Christ. Jesus is the fullness of Divine Revelation because He is God's very Word Who speaks to us in our own words, Face to face. Therefore, public revelation ends with the death of those who personally saw and heard Jesus Christ; namely, it ends with the death of the last Apostle (see Galatians 1:9 and CCC 51-73 [CCC refers to the *Catechism of the Catholic Church*, and the numbers refer to the CCC's paragraph numbers, in this case paragraphs 51 through 73]).

Oral Tradition & the Bible: Revelation was preserved almost exclusively through oral tradition for much of salvation history. Some of this oral tradition was subsequently written down and recorded in what has come to be called Sacred Scripture. In the Old Testament, this writing began with the writings of Moses or "the Law" (or the *Torah* in Hebrew). Later revelation included what Jesus called "The Law and the Prophets." Today, the Jewish people continue to follow this first series of covenants and call their Sacred Scripture the *Tanakh* in Hebrew or in English, the Hebrew Bible (they do not generally call it the Old Testament because they do not accept the New Testament). Today's Hebrew Bible does not accept all of the books as Scripture which the Catholic Church accepts as divinely inspired Old Testament books (for more on this, see the section on the Deuterocanonical Books on page 25). With the advent of Christianity, the revelation of the Old Testament is incorporated into the fullness of Divine Revelation which Jesus Christ brings to His People. Some of Jesus's words and works (and their interpretation) are written down by the Catholic Church and collected by the Church into what we call the New Testament. St. Paul makes it clear that not all "Tradition" has been written down (see 2 Thessalonians 2:15). Jesus, the fullness of Revelation, taught all things to His disciples and promised He would send the Holy Spirit Who would teach and bring all these things to recollection of the Church through the Holy Spirit (see John 14:26). Therefore, neither the Church, Tradition nor the Bible teaches that the Bible is the sole rule of faith (see John 21:25).

Inspiration and Inerrancy: Inspiration means that the Holy Spirit caused the sacred authors (the human authors), while using their natural human gifts and skills, to write down those things and only those things that He wanted them to write. This is what St. Paul meant when he said that the Scriptures are "God breathed" (see 2 Timothy 3:16). Because God is the first Author and God Who is Truth Himself, cannot deceive, there can be no error in Scripture if we understand that the purpose of Scripture is for God to reveal Himself to us for the sake of our salvation. In other words, there is absolutely no error in Scripture. If there are any assertions in Scripture that do not conform to our knowledge of history, science, etc. we can be assured the human author and the Divine Author were not asserting these things as facts but were using them as secondary elements in order to convey some other truth. For example, we might use the phrase "before the sun rose this morning" to indicate something we did before it got light. Technically, this could be declared to be a "scientific error" but we are not intending to describe the relative orbital mechanics between the earth and sun; rather we were using a common phrase to point to the time of an action that happened while it was still dark. It is not possible to assert that the Holy Spirit intended to convey error in order to teach some other truth. Scripture is inerrant because it is divinely inspired.

Transmission of Divine Revelation (CCC 74-79): Jesus said, "Go into all the world and preach the gospel to the whole creation." (Mk. 16:15). He never commanded His Apostles to go and "write" (in fact only five of the twelve Apostles wrote anything that has been preserved in Sacred Scripture). Preaching was the primary method of conveying the Gospel in the early Church. In fact, oral transmission of the faith was an absolute necessity for the first 1500 years of the Church for a number of reasons. First of all, not all the books of the New Testament were composed until many years after the Holy Spirit gives birth to the Church at Pentecost. The first books were probably not written down until perhaps the fifth decade of the first century (about twenty years after Pentecost) and by some reckonings, all of the books were not complete until around A.D. 100. Therefore, there had to be an oral tradition until at least that time. Yet another reason oral tradition was still necessary even after all the books had been written is that there was no universally accepted canon of the New Testament until the Councils of Hippo in A.D. 393 and Carthage in A.D. 397 (the first canon of the Old Testament was confirmed at the Council of Rome in AD 382). Until that time, many books not now in the New Testament were considered Scripture by some (e.g., the Letter of Clement and the Shepherd of Hermas) and other books that are now accepted as forming the canon, were rejected by some local communities (e.g., Hebrews and Revelation). It was the Magisterium of Catholic bishops who used the authoritative oral tradition passed from the Apostles to them to identify which books were written by Catholic authors and which professed the fullness of the Catholic faith without error.

These Catholic bishops then accepted these books as forming the Christian canon of the Old and New Testaments. However, even after initially establishing the canon of Scripture, the primary method of transmitting the faith still had to be oral. One of the reasons is the printing press was not invented until the 15th century and therefore, a Bible had to be handwritten. It took about a year for a monk to copy the whole Bible and so its cost was approximately a year's wage. Moreover, as the faith spread in the early Church and as Roman society collapsed, most of the Christian world's population would be illiterate and couldn't read the Bible (or any other book) anyway. From these historical facts, we can see that two things were essential which Providence provided for. First, the need for a visible, authoritative institution that could infallibly determine what was and was not part of Divine Revelation and so to discern infallibly which books to include in the canon of Scripture. Second, a universal acceptance of magisterial authority so all Christians knew where to turn to find the truth. The Magisterium of the Catholic Church must still be recognized as this universal authority despite the sad divisions in Christianity that began almost immediately after the turn of the first millennium.

Scripture, Apostolic Tradition, Magisterium: Sacred Scripture and Apostolic Tradition (oral Tradition) are the one source of God's Revelation. "The Word of God" is given to us in two distinct modes of transmission. The task of authentically interpreting both of these modes has been entrusted to the Church alone; the living, teaching office called the Magisterium (which is the Pope and all of the bishops of the world in union with him). Its authority is exercised in the name of Jesus Christ. Just like legs of a stool, all three must be kept in balance. The Magisterium serves Divine Revelation by identifying Sacred Scripture and Tradition, authoritatively interpreting them, and authoritatively applying this Revelation to the Christian life. Apostolic Tradition identifies and interprets Scripture and vice versa. If one of these legs is given undue precedence over the other two, all of Divine Revelation becomes unstable (CCC 80-100).

The Canon of Sacred Scripture: The term "canon" means "a rule." For Sacred Scripture, it refers to the formally accepted books that comprise Divine Revelation that has been written down. Sacred Scripture is a collection of books written by many human authors over many centuries, which the Church teaches to be inerrant. Scripture reveals the Mystery of God and His plan of Salvation for mankind (CCC 101-108).

Old Testament: 46 books (39 in the Protestant Bible), originally written in Hebrew, describing God's love for His people and His means of forming His family through a series of covenants. It is God's progressive revelation to His people as He prepared them for the fullness of revelation. While the Old Testament is inspired in the same way as the New Testament, it must be interpreted in light of the New Testament. "The New Testament lies hidden in the Old, and the Old Testament is unveiled in the New" (St.

24

Augustine). The Old Testament is about Jesus Christ and must be interpreted in light of Him. It is described as being comprised of four divisions (CCC 121-123).

Torah ("Law" in Hebrew) or Pentateuch ("five containers" in Greek): Torah is the first five books of the Old Testament describing the formation of God's Covenant people beginning with Adam and Eve, through the times of the Patriarchs (Abraham, Isaac, Jacob [who is renamed Israel]) until the time of Moses's death. The books of the Torah include Genesis (Gen), Exodus (Ex), Leviticus (Lev), Numbers (Num), and Deuteronomy (Deut).

Historical Books: These books describe the history of the People of God from roughly 1250 B.C. through about 130 B.C. These books are not history in the sense modern man writes history. They include the ancient approach to history along with various other types of writings we find in other books of Scripture. The historical books include Joshua (Josh), Judges (Judg), Ruth (Ruth), 1 Samuel (1 Sam), 2 Samuel (2 Sam), 1 Kings (1 Kings), 2 Kings (2 Kings), 1 Chronicles (1 Chr), 2 Chronicles (2 Chr), Ezra (Ezra), Nehemiah (Neh), Tobit (Tob), Judith (Jdt), Esther (Esth), 1 Maccabees (1 Macc), and 2 Maccabees (2 Macc).

Wisdom Books: These books are comprised of literature of the type we call proverbs, poetry, prayer and other stories revealing God's glory, the meaning of life (origin, destiny, suffering, good and evil, right and wrong) and how we are to live in light of God's revelation. The wisdom books include Job (Job), Psalms (Ps), Proverbs (Prov), Ecclesiastes (Eccl), Song of Solomon (Song), Wisdom (Wis), and Sirach/Ecclesiasticus (Sir).

Prophetic Books: These books reflect God's intervention in the affairs of His Covenant people to awaken them to their errors, to warn them of the consequences of evil behavior and to describe the glory to be found in obedience. The books include: Isaiah (Isa), Jeremiah (Jer), Lamentations (Lam), Baruch (Bar), Ezekiel (Ezek), Daniel (Dan), Hosea (Hos), Joel (Joel), Amos (Am), Obadiah (Obad), Jonah (Jon), Micah (Mic), Nahum (Nahum), Habakkuk (Hab), Zephaniah (Zeph), Haggai (Hag), Zechariah (Zech), and Malachi (Mal).

Deuterocanonical Books: The term "deutero-canon" means the "second canon." These are books of the Old Testament that the Catholic Church has recognized as part of the Old Testament since at least the 3rd century AD. Before Pentecost, when God's authority to teach authoritatively passed from Jewish authority to the Catholic Church, there was never a formal definition of the books considered to be Sacred Scripture. Various canons were used in different parts of the Jewish world. In the first century AD, Christian apologists (those who defended the Christian faith against those who argued against it, namely Jews and Greeks alike) began using the Greek translation of Old Testament books to prove to their Jewish opponents, that Jesus was indeed the promised Messiah (e.g., Isaiah 7:14). The Greek translations of these books in some cases made it difficult for the Jews to argue against the Christians points and so the Jewish Rabbis came together in what is now sometimes called the "Council of Jamnia" sometime in the second century AD. Here they declared that they would accept as Scripture, only the books found in Hebrew and only the Hebrew version of those books. Seven books and parts of two others found in the Greek translation of the Old Testament could no longer be found in Hebrew and so were excluded from the Hebrew Bible. During the Protestant Reformation, Catholics also would use works from the Deuterocanonical books to argue against the Reformers (for example, praying for the dead found in 2 Maccabees 12:44). For this reason, beginning with Martin Luther, the Protestant Reformers began to accept the Jewish canon rather than the traditional Christian canon and so removed these Old Testament books from their Bibles. The books comprising the Deuterocanonical books include: Tobit, Judith, parts of the book of Esther, The Wisdom of Solomon, Sirach, Baruch, parts of Daniel, and 1 & 2 Maccabees.

History of the Old Testament: On pages 29 and 30 are two figures that roughly show major events from the Bible and from world history that help to contextualize the time these events in each of the books of the Bible take place.

New Testament: 27 books, originally written in Greek from A.D. 50 to A.D. 100. These books reveal the fullness of God's plan of Good News for all mankind. What was revealed in veiled language in the Old Testament is uncovered and shines forth in the New Testament. (CCC 124-131)

Gospels (Greek for "Good News"): The Gospels are the heart of Scripture because they are the principle source of the life and teachings of the Incarnate Word. They are held in great esteem for this reason, but they are not any more inspired, nor can they contradict any other portion of Scripture. There are four Gospels, three are called the Synoptics because they, more or less, provide a synopsis of Jesus' life —Matthew (*Mt*), Mark (*Mk*) and Luke (*Lk*); the fourth is the Gospel of John (*Jn*). John's Gospel assumes the reader is familiar with the other Gospels and so this book is written much more in terms of the theological meaning of Jesus's life and works than the Synoptics.

Acts of the Apostles (*Acts*): Essentially, St. Luke's recounting of the history of the early Church from the Ascension until Paul's departure for Rome.

New Testament Letters: these can be seen as the pastoral application and the catechetical teaching of the Gospel. There are 21 letters in all; 14 are traditionally attributed to St. Paul: Romans (*Rom*), 1 Corinthians (*1 Cor*), 2 Corinthians (*2 Cor*), Galatians (*Gal*), Ephesians (*Eph*), Philippians (*Phil*), Colossians (*Col*), 1 Thessalonians (*1 Thess*), 2 Thessalonians (*2 Thess*), 1 Timothy (*1 Tim*), 2 Timothy (*2 Tim*), Titus (*Titus*), Philemon (*Philem*), and Hebrews (*Heb*). The 7 *Catholic Letters* are by other Apostles and

Apostolic writers written to the Universal (Catholic) Church; they include: James (*Jas*), 1 Peter (*1 Pet*), 2 Peter (*2 Pet*), 1 John (*1 Jn*), 2 John (*2 Jn*), 3 John (*3 Jn*), Jude (*Jude*).

Book of Revelation (*Rev* [also called the Apocalypse]): This is a book primarily written in the prophetic literary style of the type called apocalyptic literature. It is God's revelation describing the suffering that will occur among Christians and the glory which awaits those who persevere to the end. Catholic scholars generally describe the end of time as partially fulfilled in the first century (A.D. 70) but also pointing to the life of the Church throughout history. Revelation describes these events made present in the liturgy (particularly the Mass), and finally referring to the Second Coming of Jesus Christ at the end of time.

Interpretation of Divine Revelation. Even though the books of Scripture have the Holy Spirit as their primary Author, the human authors are also true authors. The Holy Spirit used their skills, gifts, natural knowledge, modes of speech, culture, etc. to convey His meaning. Therefore, the Holy Spirit is not only the primary Author, He is also the ultimate interpreter of all authentic Scripture. As Author, He gives Scripture its unity and coherence. As Interpreter, He acts through the Catholic Church by means of the Magisterium. Therefore, the Magisterium is the final interpreter on earth.

Literal sense: the first sense of Scripture is the literal meaning of the text; that is, the meaning intended by the human author. Understanding the literal meaning requires study to understand what the human author intended to convey to his readers. The Catholic Church teaches that authentic interpreters of Scripture must keep in mind there are many different types of writings. There is real historical information, but we must be cautious not to assume the same approach we take to writing history is the approach used in the ancient world. While there is some commonality, the ultimate purpose of history before the 17th century AD was to explain its meaning. Historical detail often took on a secondary importance if it was not directly part of the historical meaning being conveyed. There are prophetic works as well. Prophecy has its own style. It is not simply the prediction of the future, it is God speaking to His people through their own ways of speaking and thinking, in order to bring His message to them. Very often the prophets were sent when God's people, including their leaders, had gone astray and they needed more explicit direction in order to bring them back to Him. One special type of prophetic writing is called apocalyptic literature (e.g., see the Book of Ezekiel and the Book of Revelation). Here the authors use language that is difficult for us to understand today. It is very often written to people who are beginning to experience some sort of oppression. While the language may seem dark to us, it is actually encouragement that God's plan will eventually triumph.

There are many other types of literature such as poetry, proverbs, parables, allegory, epistles, midrash (explanations of the meaning based upon oral tradition), etc. Because all of these require attention first to what the human author intended, we must be attentive to the meaning of the words in the original language, the entire context of the words in the verses, the context of the verses in the chapters, the chapters in the books, and the meaning of the books in the entire canon of the Bible. Each passage therefore, must be considered as part of the unity of the whole Bible.

Spiritual Senses: Because the Holy Spirit is the first Author of Scripture, He inspires the human authors to include meaning that goes beyond what they are aware of, but which is directly connected to what they are saying. This meaning is referred to as the spiritual sense of Scripture and there are three general types. There is the allegorical or the typological meaning. This identifies Jesus Christ acting in salvation history, throughout Scripture, especially in the Old Testament. Two examples come from St. Paul who says that Adam was a type of Christ (Romans 5:14) and that the rock that followed Israel through the desert was Christ (1 Corinthians 10:4). Another spiritual sense is moral sense (also called the *tropological* sense). Scripture was not simply written to satisfy our curiosity; it was written for our instruction. The Gospel demands our response and Scripture helps to guide us in how we are to act. The final sense is the future or anagogical sense. All of the events of Scripture point to our end, which is eternal life with Christ, and to the end of time when all will be brought together again under the Headship of Jesus Christ (CCC 109-119).

Some Suggested Resources:

Catholic Encyclopedia: This is an academic overview of Scripture from the 1911 Catholic Encyclopedia - www.catholic.com/encyclopedia/scripture

Catholic Answers Tracts: This a series of articles from Catholic Answers that address a variety of topics related to the Bible:

- www.catholic.com/tracts/scriptural-reference-guide-0
- www.catholic.com/encyclopedia/canon-of-the-holy-scriptures
- www.catholic.com/tracts/scripture-and-tradition
- www.catholic.com/encyclopedia/types-in-scripture
- www.catholic.com/magazine/articles/not-by-scripture-alone
- www.catholic.com/encyclopedia/biblical-exegesis

Tim Staples on Scripture: This is an apologetic approach to understanding the Bible and the Catholic Church: www.catholic.com/blog/tim-staples/born-again-the-bible-way

Scott Hahn, Understanding Scripture: This is a very helpful book for understanding Scripture and a summary of each of the books of the Bible

Scott Hahn, A Father Who Keeps His Promises: This is a very helpful book that helps the reader to gain an overview of the major events and figures of the Old Testament in the context of their meaning and purpose in light of their fulfillment in Jesus Christ

Time Comparison of World History & Old Testament Books of the Bible

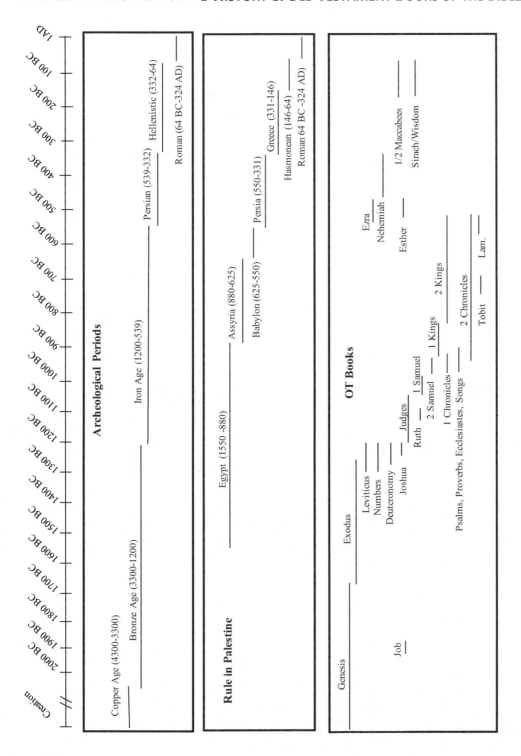

Archeological Periods

- 1AD, 100 BC, 200 BC, 300 BC, 400 BC, 500 BC, 600 BC, 700 BC, 800 BC, 900 BC, 1000 BC, 1100 BC, 1200 BC, 1300 BC, 1400 BC, 1500 BC, 1600 BC, 1700 BC, 1800 BC, 1900 BC, 2000 BC, Creation

- Persian (539-332)
- Hellenistic (332-64)
- Roman (64 BC-324 AD)
- Iron Age (1200-539)
- Bronze Age (3300-1200)
- Copper Age (4300-3300)

Rule in Palestine

- Persia (550-331)
- Greece (331-146)
- Hasmonean (146-64)
- Roman 64 BC -324 AD)
- Babylon (625-550)
- Assyria (880-625)
- Egypt (1550 -880)

OT Books

- Ezra
- Nehemiah
- Esther
- 1/2 Maccabees
- Sirach/Wisdom
- Tobit
- Lam.
- 2 Kings
- 2 Chronicles
- 1 Kings
- 1 Chronicles
- 1 Samuel
- 2 Samuel
- Judges
- Ruth
- Joshua
- Deuteronomy
- Numbers
- Leviticus
- Exodus
- Psalms, Proverbs, Ecclesiastes, Songs
- Genesis
- Job

TIME COMPARISON OF MAJOR EVENTS & BOOKS IN THE OLD TESTAMENT

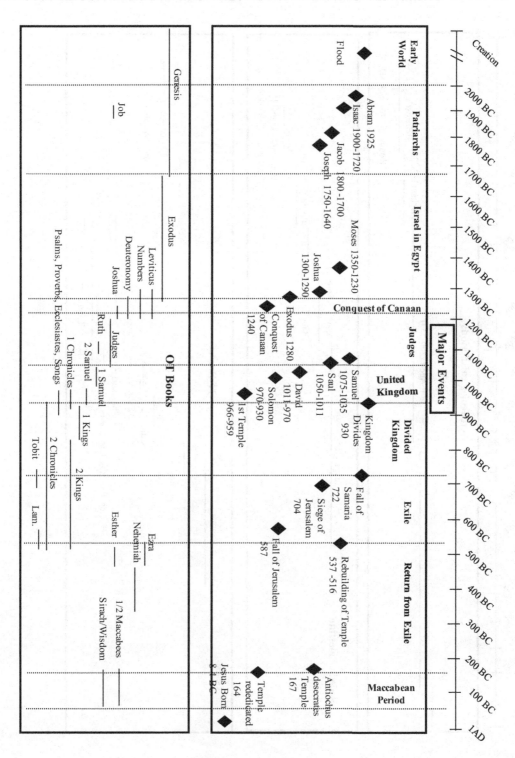

TIME COMPARISON OF MAJOR EVENTS & BOOKS IN THE NEW TESTAMENT

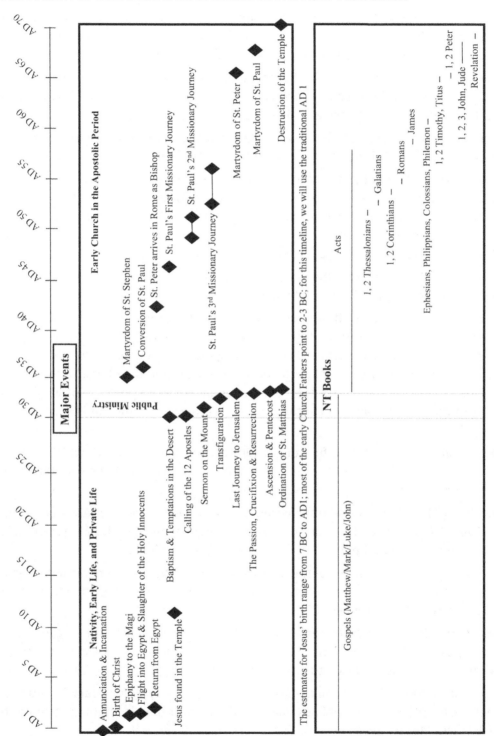

The estimates for Jesus' birth range from 7 BC to AD1; most of the early Church Fathers point to 2-3 BC; for this timeline, we will use the traditional AD 1

31

SOURCES OF SACRED TRADITION AND SOME DEFINITIONS

Catechism of the Catholic Church - A compendium of Sacred Tradition and Sacred Scripture authored by the Church's Magisterium to put Revelation in a systematic format to allow a better understanding of how the Word of God is to be understood and lived.

Development of Dogma - The fact that the understanding of Revealed Truth can deepen and be clarified through time which allows clearer definitions to be taught. Dogma can develop but it cannot change if change is to be understood as contradiction.

Doctrine - Usually used interchangeably with dogma, other times used for those teachings which are not dogmatic but must be submitted to by the faithful.

Dogma - Truths taught by Christ (or related to His Revelation), through His Church which must be held by members of the Church. Dogma is proclaimed by the Magisterium either through *ex cathedra* teachings or teachings of ecumenical councils (both are considered teachings of the Extraordinary Magisterium), or by the bishops in communion with the pope (the Ordinary Magisterium) (CCC 88-90).

Ex Cathedra - Latin for "from the Chair" of Peter. This is the most solemn form of teaching, which is declared by the Pope as infallible.

Infallibility - The negative gift by which the Holy Spirit prevents the Catholic Church from teaching error when She authoritatively proclaims a Truth regarding faith or morals and which must be definitively held. We say it is negative to distinguish it from divine inspiration where the Holy Spirit positively moves the inspired authors. In the case of infallibility, the Holy Spirit does not move the Church to teach anything positive but restrains the Magisterium from authoritatively teaching anything that is not the truth (CCC 890-892).

Magisterium - The teaching office, or teaching authority of the Church which teaches in Christ's name. Comprised of the bishops of the Church in communion with the Bishop of Rome, the pope (CCC 85-87, 888-892).

Revelation - The Word of God transmitted by two sources, Sacred (or Apostolic) Tradition and Sacred Scripture; and authoritatively interpreted by the Church's Magisterium. Public revelation ended with the death of the last Apostle (CCC 80-87).

Sacred Scripture - The Canons of the Old Testament and New Testaments authored by human writers who were inspired by the Holy Spirit and is without error when interpreted as the sacred author intended (CCC 101-141).

Sacred Tradition (also called Apostolic or Oral Tradition) - Oral Revelation revealed by Christ to His apostles which cannot change, much of which is not found explicitly in Sacred Scripture (sometimes referred to as capital "T" Tradition) (CCC 74-79, 2 Thess. 2:15).

Ecclesiastical tradition - cultural means of worship and piety which deal with liturgy, theology, devotions and disciplines that can change over time (sometimes referred to as small "t" tradition) (CCC 83).

TUTORIAL ON THE CATECHISM OF THE CATHOLIC CHURCH

What is it?: "...a statement of the Church's faith and of catholic doctrine, attested to or illumined by Sacred Scripture, the Apostolic Tradition, and the Church's Magisterium." (Apostolic Constitution *Fidei Depositum* [Deposit of Faith], paragraph 3.)

How is it organized?: The Catechism is organized into four parts:

<u>Part 1</u>: The Profession of Faith "...summarizes the gifts God gives man: as the Author of all that is good; as Redeemer; and as Sanctifier." (CCC Prologue, paragraph 14)

<u>Part 2</u>: The Sacraments of Faith "...explain how God's plan of salvation, accomplished once for all through Christ Jesus and the Holy Spirit, is made present in the sacred actions of the Church's liturgy (*Section One*), especially in the seven sacraments (*Section Two*)." (CCC Prologue, paragraph 15)

<u>Part 3</u>: The Life of Faith "...deals with the final end of man created in the image of God: beatitude, and the ways of reaching it - through right conduct freely chosen, with the help of God's law and grace (*Section One*), and through conduct that fulfills the twofold commandment of charity (love of God and neighbor), specified in God's ten commandments (*Section Two*)." (CCC Prologue, paragraph 16)

<u>Part 4</u>: Prayer in the Life of Faith "...deals with the meaning and importance of prayer in the life of believers..." ending with the sevenfold petitions of the Lord's Prayer. (CCC Prologue, paragraph 17)

How do I use it?:

1. Numbers in bold on the left are paragraph numbers, these are what is referenced in the index.
2. Italicized numbers in the right margin refer to other paragraphs which have related material to that paragraph.
3. The passages in small print indicate historical observations, apologetic material, supplementary doctrinal explanations, or quotations.
4. The sources are footnoted at the bottom. Where the term **cf.** appears, this means the footnoted sentence is not directly quoted, but paraphrased.
5. The analytical index allows one to look up subjects related to a theme. The Index of citations in the larger volume allows one to cross reference to Scripture, writings of the Early Church Fathers and other Church documents.

NOTES

SESSION 3: THE HOLY TRINITY AND CREATION

READING ASSIGNMENT

Pages 17-24: questions 33-65; pages 41-43; questions 136-146

STUDY QUESTIONS

The Holy Trinity:

- What does it mean that God is a Trinitarian God? (CCCC qq: 37, 39, 43, 44, 48)
- What does this mean for the way I understand God?
  (CCCC qq: 42, 44, 46, 47, 49, 137)
- What does God as Trinity mean for understanding life? (CCCC qq: 2, 71)

Creation:

- Why do we exist? (CCCC qq: 2, 53, 54)
- With an all Good, all knowing, all powerful God, why is there evil? (CCCC qq: 57, 58)
- What does creation mean for understanding life and its purpose?
  (CCCC qq: 54, 55, 56, 64, 65)

NOTES:

TUTORIAL ON THE TRINITY AND CREATION

The Trinity

The newness of Jesus Christ's revelation about God is that while there is one God, He is a Trinity, a tri-unity, of Persons.

Absolute Perfection: The term God speaks about His nature. Nature is the answer to the question: "what is it." There is one God, one divine nature. Divine nature is unchangeable, infinite, eternal, absolute perfection, all powerful, and all knowing. These attributes are interconnected and have practical application to our lives of knowing and loving God. They show that since God never changes, the only way our relationship with Him can change is due to our turning away and setting our will against His. Or we can turn back to God and conform our will to His will. We may need to change the way we think about God to see all His acts as acts of love.

Communion and Total Self-giving: God is a radical unity of nature, fully possessed by Three Persons. Person answers the question: "who are you?" God is "One infinite What" and "Three infinite Whos." The Names of the first two Persons reveal God is a communion of Relations. Father and Son are terms of relation. These relations are so important we pray them in the Creed. The Father "begets" (but doesn't create) the Son. The Holy Spirit "proceeds" from the Father and the Son.

Divine relations reveal communion. The Father, Son and Holy Spirit are related by one eternal act of total Self-giving. The eternal, total Self-giving of the divine Persons is love's very structure.

The Structure of Love: The divine relations among the Persons of the Trinity are the eternal, unchanging structure of love. The Father gives Himself totally to His Son in the eternal act of knowing—The Word is a Person. The Son receives Himself totally from the Father and in thanksgiving returns Himself to Him. The Son's Self-emptying act of thanksgiving (Greek: *eucharistia*), is eucharistic. This pattern is important to remember. The fruit of this reciprocal, eternal self-giving of the Father and eucharistic, self-emptying of the Son is fruitful; it is life-giving; it is a divine Person. The Holy Spirit is the Love, the Communion, which binds the Father and Son. The Holy Spirit proceeds from the Father and Son's reciprocal giving that generates the divine Word. The Holy Spirit is the eternal act of God's will.

The Divine Pattern of Creation

God's eternal act of love just described has no beginning or end. The Father always is "fathering;" the Son is always "being begotten," and the Holy Spirit is always "proceeding" and returning to the Father and Son. This cannot change. However, God can freely share His infinite, overflowing love…and He does. He creates out of nothing, having only Himself as the pattern for creation. So, creation must reflect the divine pattern of self-giving, eucharistic-self-emptying, and fruitful-life-giving love.

Creation

God created the heavens and the earth in communion with Himself, all reflecting His eucharistic, self-emptying order of divine Communion.

A Gift of Communion:

God creates from love for the sake of love. Being perfect, He doesn't need creation. He creates for the sake of sharing His love with other persons. All Three Persons, Father, Son and Holy Spirit, create the cosmos out of nothing. Everything created has God as the reason for its existence. All creation depends upon God to remain in existence.

God creates, at once, both the spiritual and the material world. He creates it in communion with Himself and with itself. The entire spiritual and material domains form a unity of created communion, a kinship as God's creatures.

The Son, the Father's Eternal Word, has a unique relationship with creation. All is created in, through and for the Son (see Jn 1:3, 10; 2 Cor 1:36; Col 1:15-16; Heb 1:2). The Son, the Eternal Word, is the model for creation.

Angels:

Angels are pure spiritual beings. They are persons created for love. They have the spiritual faculties necessary for love. They have an intellect to know God and others, and a free will so they may choose to selflessly love. They choose at the moment of their creation, after which their spiritual nature prevents change.

The name angel is their office; they are God's "messengers." Each angel is its own unique nature, so creation's spiritual dimension should be viewed as having at least as much diversity as the material order, except that the spiritual order's diversity is comprised of personal beings. Angels' purpose is to serve God by serving His creatures.

The Visible Cosmos:

Visible creation, or the material order, was created simultaneously with the spiritual order. The Book of Genesis describes creation as good. It shows a hierarchal order among creatures, with man as creation's summit. Only man is created in the image and likeness of God, only he has dominion over creation, and only he is called to rest with God on the seventh day. The Sabbath day indicates that man is already in a covenant of communion with God from the moment he is created.

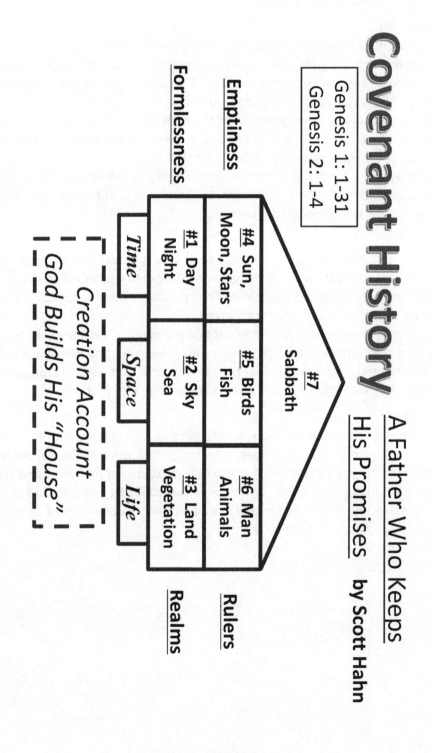

Covenant History

A Father Who Keeps
His Promises by Scott Hahn

Genesis 1: 1-31
Genesis 2: 1-4

Formlessness	Emptiness			
Time	#1 Day Night	#4 Sun, Moon, Stars	#7 Sabbath	
Space	#2 Sky Sea	#5 Birds Fish		
Life	#3 Land Vegetation	#6 Man Animals		
Realms	Rulers			

Creation Account
God Builds His "House"

THE TRINITY AND CREATION: MODEL

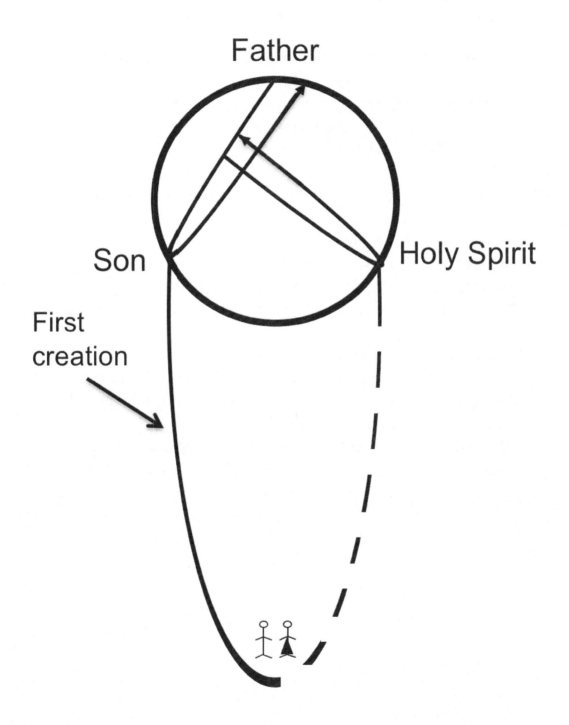

THE TRADITIONAL NINE CHOIRS OF ANGELS
(SEE ST. THOMAS AQUINAS' *SUMMA THEOLOGIAE*, IA, Q. 108, A. 5 & 6)

1st Hierarchy: They contemplate the ideas of things in God Himself and the ends of creation, and they see God most directly
- **Seraphim**: They excel in their communion with God
- **Cherubim**: They know the divine secrets super-eminently
- **Thrones**: They know the types of things in God

2nd Hierarchy: They contemplate universal causes and the universal disposition of what is to be done in creation, and govern the created order
- **Dominions**: They appoint things to be done in creation
- **Virtues**: They give the power for carrying out what is to be done
- **Powers**: They order what is to be done and how it is to be carried out

3rd Hierarchy: They contemplate the application of universal causes to their effects, and carry out the work to be done in creation
- **Principalities**: They are leaders in carrying out the things to be done ordered by the Powers
- **Archangels**: They direct the Angels in carrying out commands
- **Angels:** They are the Angels who actually carry out the commands

NOTES

NOTES

SESSION 4: MAN & THE FALL

READING ASSIGNMENT

Pages 24-27: questions 66-78

STUDY QUESTIONS

Man:

- In what two ways does man image God? (CCCC qq. 66, 67, 71)
- How does man fulfill the purpose for which God created him? (CCCC qq. 67, 71)
- How do we understand man's nature as material and spiritual? (CCCC qq. 69, 70)
- What was the original condition of man? (CCCC q. 72)

The Fall:

- What is the fall? (CCCC qq: 72, 73, 74)
- How does the fall explain the need for salvation? (CCCC qq: 75, 76, 78)
- How does it explain the challenges we face in life? (CCCC q: 77)
- How does it help me to understand the way I must change my life? (CCCC qq: 77, 297, 527)

NOTES:

TUTORIAL ON MAN AND THE FALL

Man:

Man was created last, as a special creation. He is a unity of body and spiritual soul, uniting in himself, the two orders of the cosmos, the material and the spiritual orders. In visible creation, man alone has the intellect and will necessary for a relationship of communion with God. Only man can, after the image of the Son, receive himself, and in humble, trusting, eucharistic-self-emptying, return himself to God. Man unites in his nature, visible and spiritual creation. He is in a most amazing manner, the center of all creation. So man, on behalf of all creation must return himself and creation back to God. If he refuses, all creation's communion with God will be lost.

The Four Harmonies:

When man is created, as male and female, he is in a relationship of original justice with God. The fruit of original justice for man is original grace. This relationship of harmony with God, brings about an additional three-fold harmony.

Harmony with God results in interior harmony, interpersonal harmony with others, and harmony with the rest of creation. Interior harmony means that man can act completely freely, with complete control over his passions. Then he can authentically love with little effort. Interpersonal harmony means that there is no conflict between persons. Harmony with sub-personal creation means that nothing in creation would harm man; rather, it would serve him.

Image & Likeness:

Man is the only creature in visible creation made in God's image and likeness. Traditionally, the emphasis of the image has been on man's intellect and will, which have their origin in the soul. Yet, recently attention has turned to St. Thomas Aquinas' observation that the body also permits man to reflect God's image—even more perfectly than angels. Let's look at how both the soul and body image God.

Intellect and will:

The intellect is the faculty by which the human person exercises his reason, by which he searches for, and comes to know and understand truth. The will is the faculty permitting him to choose freely the good and the true. These two faculties belong to the spiritual order, even if their operation requires the cooperation of the body.

These faculties separate us from lower animals, revealing we are persons. Divine Persons possess the divine intellect and will. Angelic persons possess an angelic intellect and will. These two faculties are ordered to love; the ultimate purpose of the intellect is to know the other and the purpose of the will is to love the other.

In visible creation, human beings are the only creatures with an intellect and will; therefore, only humans are persons. In visible creation, only human persons can enter into communion, that is into relationships of selfless love, with God, with angels and with each other.

Union of spirit and matter:

Humans are not pure spirit; we are a unity of nature, body and soul. We share with lower animals many features that come with having a body. Our bodies are made of matter and this connects us intimately with the rest of visible creation. But we also are spiritual beings because of our spiritual souls. The soul intimately joins us to the spiritual dimension of creation.

However, it is important to understand the oneness of human nature. Our body-soul unity should not be envisioned as giving us two natures, or even as giving us two parts of one nature. The unity of body and soul is so intimate that the soul seamlessly permeates the entire body.

When you see the body, you see the soul. When you touch the body, you touch the soul. The human person, a unity of body-soul, is sacred and so the body is sacred. The soul gives the body its existence, its shape, its self-directed growth, and its motion. The soul was never intended to exist without its body.

Man seamlessly unites material creation with spiritual creation, making him the center of the created order. Man is therefore uniquely suited to mediating between spirit and matter. He is able, through his actions, to affect all creation. The body is essential to being human and is essential to one way we image God (i.e., procreation).

Sex differences:

St. Thomas indicated that angels are more like God in "what" they are, pure spirit. However, he said man is more like God in that man can beget man in a way analogous to God the Father's begetting of God the Son. This is an important Trinitarian insight that illuminates the great dignity of sex differences, of marriage, and of family. These are relationships of communion. The total self-giving of parents is to reflect the total Self-giving of God; it is to be fruitful and life-giving.

Sex differences have their origin in God. The complementarity of man and woman reflects the perfect complementarity in God. The complementarity of sex difference involves the entirety of the human person, who is a spiritual person, making him a man or woman. Man is configured according to his sex from gross anatomy down to the level of gametes and everything in between (e.g., brain structure, bone density, fatty tissue distribution, emotionally, psychologically, and spiritually). One's sex is at the heart of one's personal identity; this can't be changed. Sex difference configures the way one loves.

Original Integrity:

Man was made for relationships of communion with God and with other created persons. The faculties of the intellect and will are at the center of all relationships because they are necessary for love. However, the entire person, body-soul is involved, including the "affects" which are those things that "affect" us. They are the appetites and emotions which move us to pursue goods or avoid evils, and reward us when we choose goods. Let's look at how these three are interrelated in the soul.

We were originally created in communion with God and we were permeated with original grace. The "model of the soul" (page 53) is meant to illustrate this original integration. The three spheres depict the integration among the intellect, will and affects. The different sizes indicate the intensity with which we experience each (e.g., our affects tend to be the greatest influence on the way we experience an event and on the way we act).

The order is the hierarchy before the fall. The most important point here is that the affects should always be subordinated to the intellect. Our affects are powerful "truth-tellers" in that they tell us about the presence of an apparent good or evil and try to move us toward goods and away from evils. They are rarely in error about apparent goods. However, they cannot determine if the good or evil is authentically good or evil for us.

Circumstances can make an apparent good (e.g., a piece of chocolate cake) not good for us (e.g., we have already had two pieces). Only the intellect can distinguish between apparent and authentic goods and so the affects must always follow the intellect. This was always the natural case in original grace; the affects always obeyed the intellect and will.

The last aspect of the model we should point out is that spheres do not naturally balance on one another. There is a shaft through the center of the spheres by which grace (the gray line) enters the soul to keep them balanced. The shaft reflects the fact that we are made to receive grace, and that we need grace for our faculties to operate in an integrated manner. This is man's natural state, which made communion a natural reality.

The Fall

Created persons, both angelic and human, are the only creatures with the capacity for relationships of communion with God because only they are persons. Persons alone possess the spiritual faculties (i.e., intellect and will) which permit them to choose selfless love freely or to choose freely an existence of selfishness (which leads to spiritual enslavement).

Let's return to our communion model and recall that all creation must be a reflection of God because He is the only possible archetype for all creation. Creation reflects its special relationship to the Son meaning that it is to receive itself and in trust, thanksgiving and love, to return itself to God completing an act of communion.

Creatures who are not persons do this simply by being what God created them to be; they cannot choose anything else. Angels and man are the only creatures who have this task, to trust God and in humility and thanksgiving to give themselves back totally to Him.

The Angels' Fall:

At the moment of their creation, angels were given all they needed to know about God and creation and were to choose to follow the pattern of the Son, to return themselves totally to God or to refuse love and communion.

Scripture testifies that Satan and other angels with him irrevocably refused communion with God. There is a tradition that Satan was told God's plan was that angels would serve man and that God would become one of them.

Satan's response was *non serviam*, I will not serve. Basing themselves on the Book of Revelation (Rev 12:4-9), some Fathers of the early Church taught that a third of the angels followed Satan.

Satan and his minions now act to thwart God's plan for man's salvation, but their power is finite. They cannot win, but out of hatred for God and man they do all they can to harm man spiritually and indirectly, physically. Fallen angels, like men who reject God's love, are still part of God's creation and so are permitted their evil acts until the final coming.

Man's Communion Lost:

Our first parents were brought into a world which was in communion with God but evil had already had its entry through the fallen angels. Like the angels, Adam and Eve were given the task to be like God after the pattern of the Son. Through Satan's temptation, in the imagery of the ancient serpent, they elected their own way to be like God. They refused God's will and chose to be "like" God but without Him. In one sense, they attempted "to create" a world without God, which is a world opposed to Him, by attempting to "know" evil.

East of Eden:

The Book of Genesis depicts the separation of man from communion with God as being cast out of the Garden of Eden. Man now lives east of Eden deprived of original grace and the life God had intended for him. Man and nature were intended for grace, and both have now lost it. Without this grace to pass to his children, every human now lives east of Eden and suffers the consequences of original sin.

The Effects of the Fall

Every person born is now born as a child of Adam and Eve. According to our model, we are now in a "relational dead end." An infinite breach has been opened between God and man and we now suffer its effects. We are going "nowhere!" nowhere good, anyway. We can no longer get to the place for which God made us.

God is the Author of life and so Adam and Eve's choosing "not God" means they have chosen "not life" and "not love." Our first parents' choice to try to be their own gods brings sin and death into the world. Spiritually they died immediately, the life of God left them. Eventually death would also enter their bodies through sickness, injury and old age.

Original sin for the children of Adam and Eve is not our personal sin, but it has wounded our human nature by depriving it of what it needs for harmonious living. The Book of Genesis depicts four effects of this first sin (see Gen 3:16-18).

Four Disharmonies:

Earlier we indicated that our communion with God was the source of three other harmonies in the world. The disharmonies model (pg. 55) shows how sin has resulted in disharmony. Disharmony with God results in an interior disharmony resulting in concupiscence. Concupiscence means we can no longer easily say "no" to ourselves. This of course, leads quickly to disharmony with other persons.

Yet, the disharmony that comes from lost grace includes the loss of harmony with all creation. Genesis depicts this last disharmony as the ground's becoming cursed and turning against man (Gen 3:17-18). Let's now look at the effects of concupiscence on the soul's faculties using our earlier "snowman" model.

Disgraced:

The effect of concupiscence on human experience can be shown by the collapsed snowman (page 56). Without grace holding the soul's faculties in the proper integration, the affects (the emotions and appetites) now function as if they were on the same level as the intellect and will. That is, they no longer easily obey reason, though they are still made to do so.

Before the fall, the affects did not need to be trained. They would not persist in trying to move the intellect and will to pursue a good if the intellect had already determined it to be only an apparent good. The intellect would not have easily erred in discerning between apparent and authentic goods, as is now the case.

The dis-graced soul in which the affects have not been trained now will have a struggle when presented with, say, our third piece of chocolate cake. The appetite will continue to demand the person obtain the good it has become aware of. It is the same good as last time we said yes to it, but the affects cannot determine that it is no longer good for us. This is the job of the intellect. We can see this struggle in a spoiled child who throws a tantrum when the demands of his appetite are not fulfilled. As we age, we may hide this struggle but it is still there.

The soul's integration can be restored to some degree. He who reintegrates his snowman we say has character or virtue. Virtue is built by repeatedly and consistently saying "no" to our appetite's demands for only apparent goods. We never can completely overcome concupiscence through human effort alone. If we allow ourselves to develop seriously bad habits, which are vices or even addictions, the path back to self-mastery can be a very difficult or even impossible without supernatural help.

Love is now a task:

We are made for communion. We find our fulfillment only in giving ourselves totally to God and selflessly to others. However, we cannot give what we do not first possess. East of Eden, we cannot love as we want to. Learning to love as we were made is now hard work. In order to say "yes" to God and to the good of others, we must train our affects to obey when we say "no" to apparent goods. Developing the strength to love heroically means first developing self-mastery through a life of virtue.

The Order of Creation

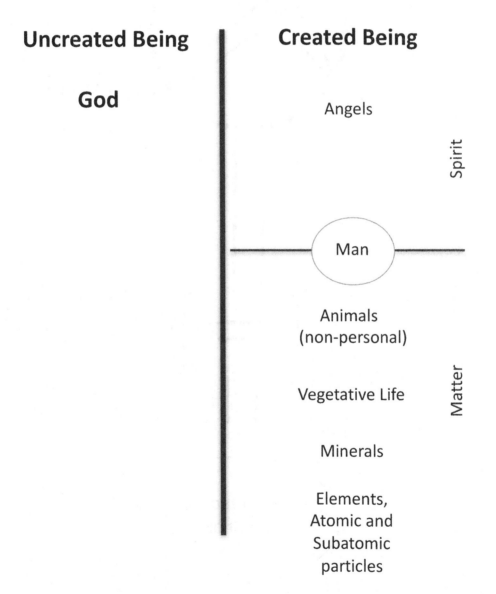

Uncreated Being   **Created Being**

God   Angels

                                            Spirit

                        Man

                        Animals
                        (non-personal)

                                            Matter

                        Vegetative Life

                        Minerals

                        Elements,
                        Atomic and
                        Subatomic
                        particles

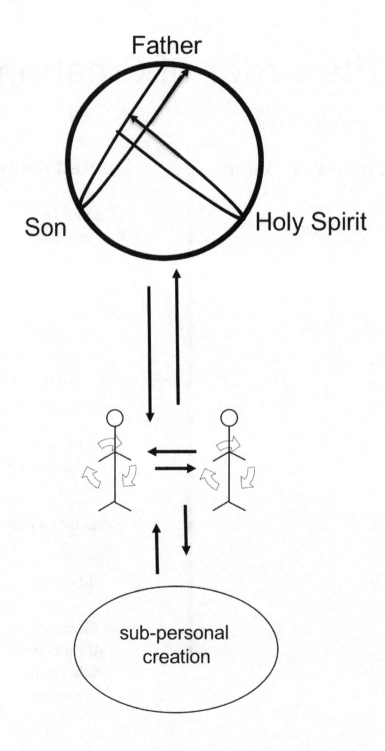

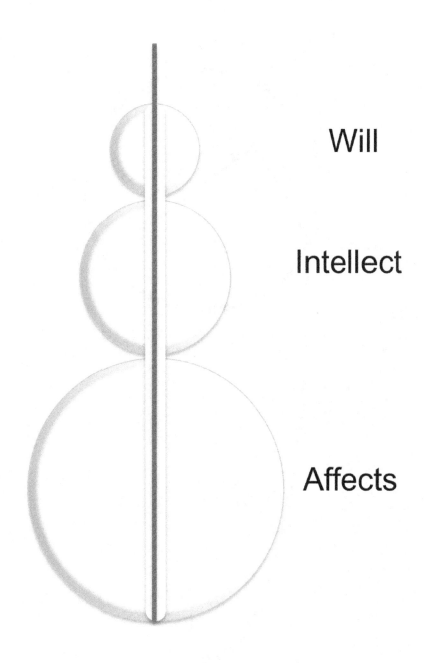

Will

Intellect

Affects

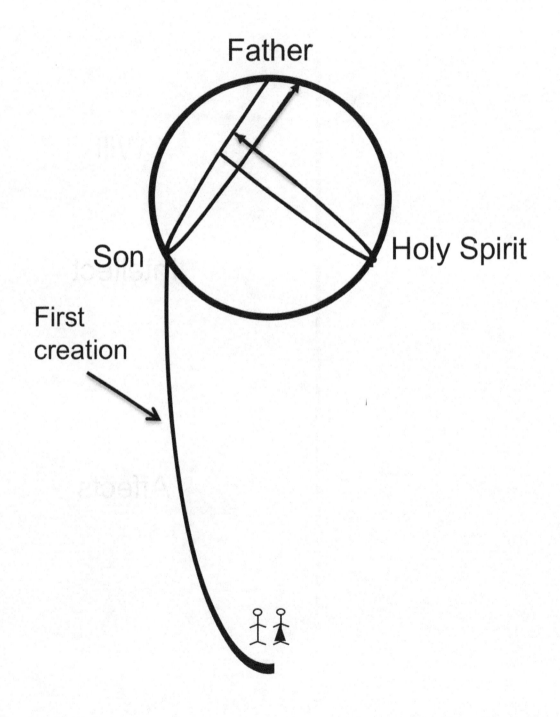

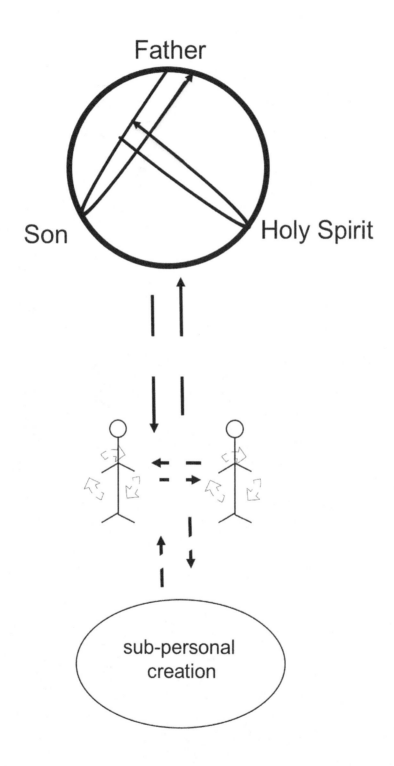

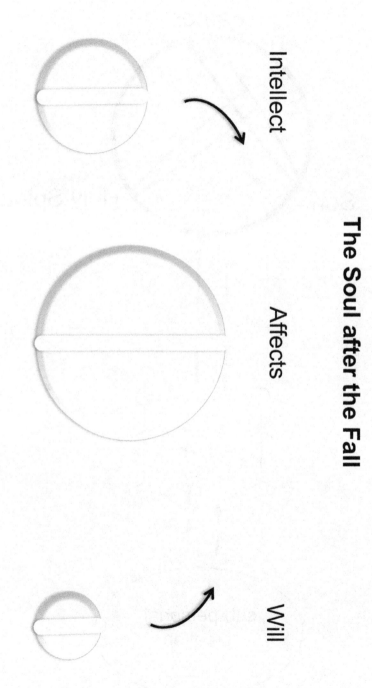

Intellect

Affects

Will

The Soul after the Fall

NOTES

SESSION 5: SALVATION HISTORY, THE INCARNATION, & CHRIST'S PUBLIC MINSTRY

READING ASSIGNMENT

Pages 27-35: questions 79-111

STUDY QUESTIONS

Salvation History:

- What does it mean that God calls man into a covenant? (CCCC qq: 7, 79, 51, 340)
- What does the progression of Old Testament covenants indicate about our relationship with God? (Handouts)
- What does Jesus' fulfillment of all the Covenant promises indicate about the Church today? (CCCC qq: 79, 80, 81, 82)
- What does salvation history teach us for our own spiritual development? (Handouts)

The Incarnation:

- What does the union of man and God in Jesus Christ mean for our personal intimacy with God? (CCCC qq: 85, 87, 101)
- What does it mean for us that Jesus Christ is truly God and truly Man? (CCCC qq: 87, 89, 90, 91, 92)
- What does God becoming a baby and entrusting Himself to the care of a woman tell us about the character of the relationship He calls us into? (CCCC qq: 95, 96, 97, 98, 99, 100, 103)

Christ's Public Ministry:

- Why was Jesus baptized by John in the Jordan? (CCCC q. 105)
- What do we learn from Jesus' temptations? (CCCC q. 106)
- What do Jesus' signs and miracles reveal about the kingdom? (CCCC q. 108)
- What do we learn from the Transfiguration? (CCCC 110)

NOTES:

Covenant History

A Father Who Keeps His Promises   by Scott Hahn

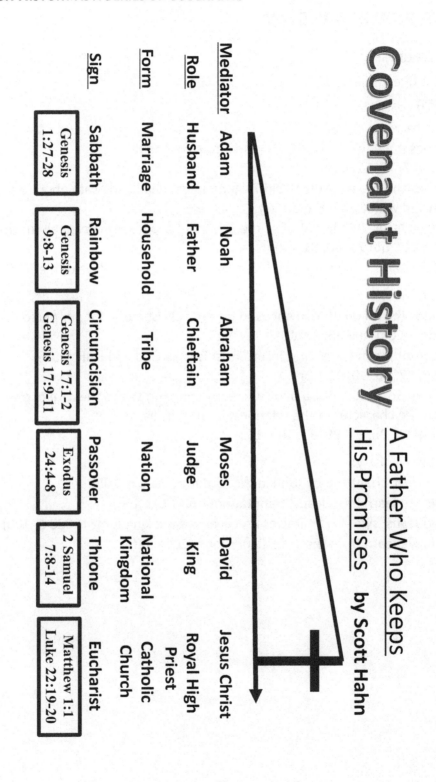

	Adam	Noah	Abraham	Moses	David	Jesus Christ
Mediator	Adam	Noah	Abraham	Moses	David	Jesus Christ
Role	Husband	Father	Chieftain	Judge	King	Royal High Priest
Form	Marriage	Household	Tribe	Nation	National Kingdom	Catholic Church
Sign	Sabbath	Rainbow	Circumcision	Passover	Throne	Eucharist
	Genesis 1:27-28	Genesis 9:8-13	Genesis 17:1-2 Genesis 17:9-11	Exodus 24:4-8	2 Samuel 7:8-14	Matthew 1:1 Luke 22:19-20

SUMMARY OF SALVATION HISTORY

Covenant versus Contract: A contract is an agreement that normally exchanges property, goods or services. A covenant is the formation of a family, an exchange of "persons" sealed by the swearing of an oath. In a contract, you say "this is yours and that is mine;" while in a covenant you say "I am yours and you are mine." God brings man into a family relationship through His covenant.

Adam	God's covenant with the smallest unit: Marriage
	Covenant Role: Husband
	Covenant Sign: Sabbath
	Genesis: 1:27-28
Noah	God's covenant with: Family
	Covenant Role: Father
	Covenant Sign: Rainbow
	Genesis: 9:8-11
Abraham	God's covenant with multiple families and households: Tribe
	Covenant Role: Chieftain
	Covenant Sign: Circumcision
	Genesis 12:1-3
Moses	God's covenant with 12 tribes of Israel: Nation
	Covenant Role: Judge
	Covenant Sign: Passover
	Exodus 19:4-6; 24:4-11
David	God's covenant with several nations: Kingdom
	Covenant Role: King
	Covenant Sign: Throne
	2 Samuel 7:9-12
Jesus	God's covenant with World-Wide International Catholic Church: (One, Holy, Catholic and Apostolic) Family of God, Communion of Saints
	Covenant Role: Royal High Priest
	Covenant Sign: Eucharist
	Matthew 1: 1
	Luke 22:19-20

SALVATION HISTORY EXPANDED

Adam

Genesis 1:27-28 – *God created man….male and female he created them*; sex and marriage is established by God, not by man

Mt 19:6 – *"What God has joined together, let no man put asunder;"* Pharisees questioned Jesus about divorce, Jesus referenced Genesis

Gen 2:25 – *naked yet they felt no shame*; the way we were meant to be

Gen 3:7 – *eyes were opened, realized they were naked*; nature has fallen

Gen 3:10 – *"I was afraid, because I was naked;"* ruptured relationship

Gen 3:21 – *Lord God made leather garments*; God still provides for us

Noah

Gen 5:8 – *But Noah found favor with the Lord*; covenant line continues

Gen 6:18 – *But with you I will establish my covenant*; covenant will be renewed with Noah, his wife, their three sons (Shem, Ham and Jepheth) and their wives

Gen 9:8-11 – *The great flood*; alienation from God's covenant

Gen 9:17 – *Rainbow is the sign of the covenant*; covenant renewal

Abraham

Gen 12:1-3 – *God sends Abram forth from the land of his kinsfolk and his father's house* with promise: *I will make you great nation, great name, blessing for nations*; three-fold covenant promise

Gen 15:7-21 – *God will give Abraham land to be a great nation;* 1st promise

Gen 17:1-21 – *God will make Abraham father of royal dynasty;* 2nd promise

Gen 22:15-18 – *God will bless all men thru Abraham's seed;* 3rd promise

Gen 14:17-18 – *Abram returns in victory giving Melchizedek, King of Salem, a tithe and Melchizedek offers bread and wine and blesses Abraham*; passing of covenant line through blessing

Gen 15:5 – *God tells Abram to look up at the sky and count the stars but it is daylight (see verse 12)*; God calls Abraham to a commitment of faith

Gen 17:2 – *Between you and me I will establish my covenant*

Gen 17:10-11 – *Circumcise foreskin of every male*; covenant sign

Gen 21:2-3 – *90-year-old Sarah becomes pregnant and bears Isaac*; God can bring life where it looks impossible, His promises can be trusted

Gen 22:7-8 – *Abraham is called to sacrifice his son*; this is a call to trust God completely

Gen 22:11-13 – *Angel to Abraham "Do not sacrifice your son;"* God provides Sacrifice at Mt Moriah – outside of Salem – later Jerusalem; God will provide a lamb as a "type" of Christ now and in the fullness of time, His Son

Gen 35:22-23 – *Sons of Jacob, Abraham's grandsons are now the Twelve Tribes of Israel (Jacob's new name)*; the Old Testament "church" is formed

Moses

Ex 2:5 – *Moses rescued from the Nile by Pharaoh's daughter*

Ex 2:15 – *Moses fled to the land of Midian*; preparation for mission

Ex 3:4 to 4:17 – *In burning bush, the God of Abraham, Isaac and Jacob*; God reveals His covenant name and begins its renewal

Ex 4:24-26 – *Zipporah circumcises their son saving Moses*; the covenantal sign of circumcision is essential for covenant

Ex 12:7 – *Blood of the lamb on doorposts and lintel*; Passover

Ex 12:11 – *It is the "Passover" of the Lord, loins girt, staff in hand*; annual celebration of covenant event is mandated

Ex: 24:6-8 – *Sacrifice, blood sprinkled on altar and people*; covenant is sealed with the blood of Sacrifice

David

1 Sam 17:41-51 – *David kills Goliath with sling shot and one stone*; God is with David in a special way

1 Sam 21:4-7 – *Bread of the presence that only priests may eat is eaten by David and his men*; David is prefigured as Christ, high priest

2 Sam 5:4 – *David is anointed king over Judah, then all Israel and Judah in Jerusalem*; David is the forerunner of the Messiah, Jesus Christ

2 Sam 6:14-15 – *David dances/leaps for joy before the Ark of Covenant into Jerusalem*; prefigures the entry of Jesus into Jerusalem

2 Sam 7:12-13 – *When David rests, God will raise up his heir from his loins*; promise the Messiah will be King in the line of David

1 Kings 2:2-4 – *David's last words to his son Solomon*; passing of covenant line

Jesus Christ

Mt 1:1 – *Genealogy of Jesus Christ*; Jesus as son of David, son of Abraham fulfills one requirement to be Messiah

Lk 2:21-22 – *Jesus' circumcision 8 days following law of Moses*; obedience to the covenant law while it is still Old Covenant

Lk 3:23-38 – *Genealogy of Jesus from Joseph back to Adam*; hint that covenant is expanding to now include all humanity

Jn 11:55-57 – *Last Passover meal*; Old Testament Passover will be transformed into New Testament Eucharist

Mt 26:28 – *Blood of the covenant is shed for the forgiveness of sins*; fulfills what Moses prefigured in Exodus 24

1 Cor 11:25 -- *This cup is the new covenant in my blood*; Paul confirms that Eucharist is Real Presence of Jesus Christ in Bread and Wine

Mt 28:19-20 – *Baptizing...in the name of the Father, Son and Holy Spirit... teaching them...all I have commanded you...I am with you always, until the close of the age*; mission of the Church is to bring all mankind into communion with Christ through Baptism

TUTORIAL ON THE INCARNATION

The Incarnation

We ended the last session with man's loss of communion with God. Man ruptured this communion because he refused to entrust himself to God's provident love. He trusted himself rather than God, turning inward rather than giving himself totally to Him. Believing he could be "like God" without Him, Adam wounded himself and all of creation.

Man's breaking communion has opened an infinite breach. He must return himself to God in an act of total self-giving reflecting the Son's eternal return to the Father. We must imitate the Son and return ourselves completely back to the Father but the Fall leaves us incapable. We need an infinite Person to bridge this infinite gap. God the Son must become the God-Man, Jesus Christ. Another way of saying this is that man now must be able to love infinitely if communion is to be restored. God becomes man so we may love infinitely.

Incarnation of love; a new creation:

Venerable Fulton J. Sheen had a little vignette he used to explain the intimate relationship between creation and redemption in the Incarnate Son. He began by imagining creation as a great symphony with God as the Conductor. Suddenly, two of the members of the orchestra purposefully play a sour note. What shall the Conductor do?

He could ignore the sour note and keep on conducting as if nothing happened but this would not be just to Him or to the two playing the sour note. The other option would be to take that sour note and make it the first note of a new symphony. God takes the second option after man rebels. He takes the sour note of man's sin, his refusal of love through self-surrender to God. This rupture of God's first creation through Adam's sin becomes the first note of a new symphony. The Incarnation inaugurates a new creation.

St. John reveals that the advent of Jesus Christ should be viewed as a new creation. He starts his Gospel with "In the beginning" (Jn 1:1), an allusion to the first verse of the Bible, which is the story of the first creation. If one looks closely he will see that John then lays out 7 days of a new creation week. Three times John repeats the phrase "the next day" (Jn 1:29, 35, 43) and then announces "on the third day" the wedding feast at Cana (Jn 2:1). This wedding feast on the "third day" points to Easter Sunday, the day of Christ's Resurrection. This third day is also the seventh day of the new creation week making Sunday the new Sabbath. The wedding feast at Cana is Jesus' first sign in which the "good wine" points to the Eucharist. The Book of Revelation suggests Cana's wedding feast is fulfilled in the wedding feast of the Lamb (Rev 19). We celebrate the Lamb's wedding feast in every Mass, which is the work of the Cross and the Resurrection (Rev 5:6).

Man refused to return himself to God in the first creation and so rendered himself unable to love God effectively; incapable of returning to God. To remedy this, Infinite Love comes to earth as a new born baby Boy conceived by the power of the Holy Spirit and born of the Virgin Mary. Jesus Christ, the God-Man, came to do for man what Adam had refused.

Humanity reunites with Divinity:

The Incarnation is the eternal Son of God assuming a complete human nature, a body-soul unity. The Son unites Himself so intimately to His humanity that in Jesus Christ there is one divine Person Who eternally possesses divine nature and within creation fully possesses His human nature. Jesus Christ is one divine Person, fully God and fully man.

The Son is fully united to His human nature from the moment of Jesus' conception at the Annunciation of the Angel Gabriel to Mary (Lk 1:26-35). He is fully God and fully Man while he grows in Mary's womb, when He is born into the world on Christmas Day, nursed at His mother's breast and remains the God-Man when He dies on the Cross. Jesus Christ is Communion in Himself because in His Person He reunites humanity with divinity and restores a communion which had been lost since Adam's and Eve's rebellion.

Communion restored in Christ:

In Jesus Christ, humanity returns to the communion of the Father, Son and Holy Spirit because of the Son's assumed human nature. Yet, for this communion to be shared with men more was needed. Man's total gift of himself back to the Father must still be made.

SESSION 6: THE PASCHAL MYSTERY & THE CHURCH

READING ASSIGNMENT

Pages 35-41: questions 112-135; pages 42-50: questions 140-176; page 67: questions 218-220

STUDY QUESTIONS

The Paschal Mystery:
- What is the Paschal Mystery? (CCCC qq: 112-135)
- Why is it the center of the mystery of Redemption? (CCCC qq: 112, 118, 119, 126)
- What does it show us about love? (CCCC qq: 122, 123)

The Church:
- Why is the Church necessary for salvation? (CCCC qq: 143, 144, 145, 149, 150, 152)
- Does a Church make sense based upon human nature and Salvation history? (CCCC qq: 151, 153, 156, 158, 159)
- What does a Church indicate for who God is and who we are? (CCCC qq: 156, 157, 158, 159)

NOTES:

TUTORIAL ON THE PASSION AND THE CHURCH

The Passion

Let's return to Sheen's vignette and that sour note. Original sin was refusing total self-giving, rejecting his image of the Son. That sin will soon be repeated but as a new note and with redemptive effect.

Total Self-gift and the Cross:

The logic of the new note becomes apparent in our *Communion* model (page 71). Jesus' entire life is a manifestation of obedient love for His Father. He told His disciples that His food was to do the will of His Father (Jn 4:34) in contrast to the first Adam who ate the fruit of the tree in disobedience (Gen 3:6).

What the Son does eternally, He now accomplishes within time in His Passion and death. Jesus' obedient, total Self-giving love is manifested most perfectly in Sheen's sour note (see page 64). Adam's sin of refusing obedient, total self-giving love is now repeated by the Jewish leaders.

The leaders' sin is the most grave possible—killing our God. But this sin is also the act by which the obedient Son, the infinite Man, returns Himself completely to the Father. He gives the Father His Body and Soul, His human life. In this act of total Self-giving love, Jesus repairs what Adam had ruptured.

Jesus act of total Self-giving love restores communion with God for the rest of humanity who will follow Him. He makes death, which enters creation in Original sin, a door to eternal life through which His disciples must pass. But not just any death will do. A saving death is one united to Christ's death on the Cross. We must die to the fallen first creation by uniting ourselves to Christ in His offering of love to the Father. Jesus warns His disciples that if we are to follow Him we must first count the cost, then take up our Cross and give ourselves to the Him (Lk 14:27-33). But why must it be the Cross?

The Horror of Sin:

The first reason is the Cross reveals to us the horror of sin. Jesus' Passion shows us what sin really looks like. If there is any doubt about its horror, we might read Isaiah 52-53. We can also get a clearer view of sin's horror by reading *A Doctor at Calvary* or viewing Mel Gibson's *Passion of the Christ*. Yet, as much as the Cross reveals the horror of rejecting God, it also reveals love.

The Manifestation of Love:

The depth of God's love is unimaginable. Jesus' last words before dying, while suffering unimaginable pain, are not words of condemnation but of forgiveness. Love hung upon the Cross for us (Rom 5:6-8). But the Cross was not God's choice. It was Satan who chose the instrument of his own undoing. Satan tempted men to put God to death on the Cross but in so doing he unwittingly helps Man to do what Adam refused. This act of sin didn't further separate man from God but because it was Jesus' act of obedient, total Self-giving love, it reconciles him. Because of the Cross, where sin abounds, grace abounds all the more (Rom 5:18-21). Satan has become the agent of his own undoing. The more he succeeds in tempting men to sin, he assists its reconciliation with God. The Cross reveals love to be stronger than death; human love now defeats evil.

Body of Christ

We ended the previous session with Jesus' defeat of sin and death through His love on the Cross. We now turn to the historical events which completed Christ's return to the Father. We then will be ready to discuss how each person may be incorporated into the fruit of His Passion; that is, the Church.

Resurrection & Ascension:

After His death on the Cross, Jesus descended into the abode of the dead where He preached the Good News to the souls there awaiting entry into heaven. For three days the earth lay silent. The Light of the World was extinguished, but death could not hold Him. Death is separation from God due to sin. On the third day, He rose from the dead in His Resurrected body, infused with the Holy Spirit. Christ's death was an act of total Self-giving love. He chose the Father and in so choosing, won resurrected life for Himself and for His faithful disciples. His glorified humanity is now so permeated by the Spirit, it takes on new abilities.

The Resurrection opens the path for every human person to be transformed in the life of the Spirit. Yet, if we return to our communion model below, we see Jesus still had to ascend back to the Father. He had told His disciples before His Passion that it was necessary He return to the Father if the Holy Spirit, the other Paraclete, was to come (Jn 16:5-7).

Pentecost: Incorporation into the Body:

Fifty Days after the Resurrection, the Holy Spirit descends upon the disciples in the Upper Room, incorporating them into Christ's Body, the Church. The Church is organically structured; it has a hierarchy as does a body (1 Cor 12:12-31). In this body, Christ is the Head, the Holy Spirit is the Soul, and His disciples are its manifold members.

The gray arrow in the model (page 71) indicates how each member is incorporated into Christ's Body, the new creation brought about by the Incarnation (2 Cor 5:17; Gal 6:15). In Baptism we enter new life but only through the Cross. Baptism unites us into Christ's death. In this, we also rise with Him and are made one in Him (Rom 6:3-10), and one with one another (Rom 7:4). We enter into the life of the Trinity (Jn 17:20-23), the Communion for which we are made. The magnification of the line indicates that one's incorporation into the Church is perfected when we are completely conformed to Christ (the middle line). The outside lines show the limits after which our failure to love adequately puts us outside of the Church (i.e., mortal sin). The only way to heaven is in union with Christ; in a state of grace.

The Bride of Christ

The Church is the Body of Christ, which is a one flesh union of Head and members. This one flesh union is also reflected in the image of Jesus Christ the Bridegroom, and the Church His Bride (Jn 3:29). The Old Testament Prophets revealed this nuptial relationship between God and His Church.

***Betrothal Marriage in the Old Testament*:**

As the Incarnation nears, the dominant image for God's relationship with the Old Testament Church is the Bridegroom. In every case in which God is presented as the Bridegroom, He is simultaneously Israel's Redeemer. Spousal love is equated with redemptive love. Hosea points out the type of marriage that still exists before Christ; he says it is a betrothal marriage (Hos 2:19-20).

A betrothal marriage at that time was like an engagement but more solemn. The parents would marry their children to one another, but they would not come together until both were of age. This would happen in a weeklong wedding feast, in the midst of which the marriage would be consummated.

***Consummation in Christ*:**

The early Church saw the consummation in Christ's Passion. St. Augustine employed St. Paul's identification of Jesus as the new Adam. St. Augustine said that just as the first Adam's bride was taken from his side from a deep sleep, Jesus, the second Adam, brings forth His Bride during His deep sleep of death.

John's Gospel shows emphatically that what comes forth from the Bridegroom's side from the Cross is not just Blood, but Water and Blood. St. Augustine points out these are the signs of entry into the Church, the signs of Baptism and the Eucharist. The Church, the Bride of Christ comes forth from His side as Blood and Water, within the wedding feast of the Paschal Lamb. Jesus' marriage to His Church is consummated on the Cross.

Paul indicates that Jesus' relationship to the Church is the same relationship as human marriage (see Eph 5:23-32). Jesus gives His flesh on the Cross and in the Eucharist for His Bride-Body to sanctify Her. Husbands are to do likewise.

The Church is communion with Jesus Christ. In Her, we are united with Christ and so we are united with the Trinity and become partakers of the divine nature (2 Pet 1:4). Only in the Bride do we have communion with the Bridegroom. As the Church Father, St. Cyprian of Carthage, said: he cannot have God as Father who will not have Church as Mother. Unity with Christ is unity with the Church; the only path to the Father.

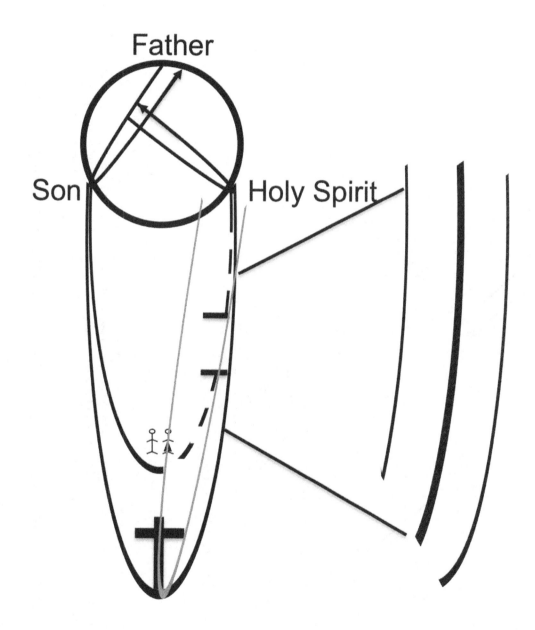

Unity with Christ's One, Holy, Catholic, Apostolic Church

One: Jesus founded only one Church, visible on earth by those in Communion with the Successor of St. Peter (see Matt 16:18). How do we understand the relationship of those other Christian communities who are not in full communion with the one Church. Every Baptized Christian is in some imperfect communion with the Catholic Church. There are two aspects of the communion: a) visible (or formal) communion based upon one's profession of and adherence to the fullness of the faith; b) non-visible (moral) communion based upon their state of perfection in love (holiness). The following two charts can help to demonstrate this:

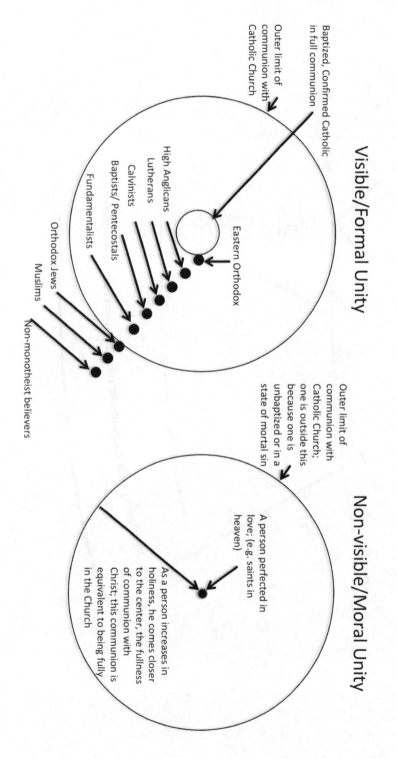

Visible/Formal Unity

Baptized, Confirmed Catholic in full communion

Outer limit of communion with Catholic Church

High Anglicans
Lutherans
Calvinists
Baptists/ Pentecostals
Fundamentalists

Orthodox Jews
Muslims
Non-monotheist believers

Eastern Orthodox

Non-visible/Moral Unity

Outer limit of communion with Catholic Church; one is outside this because one is unbaptized or in a state of mortal sin

A person perfected in love; (e.g. saints in heaven)

As a person increases in holiness, he comes closer to the center; the fullness of communion with Christ; this communion is equivalent to being fully in the Church

NOTES

SESSION 7: THE COMMUNION OF SAINTS & THE BLESSED VIRGIN MARY

READING ASSIGNMENT

Pages 51-56: questions 177-199

STUDY QUESTIONS

Communion of Saints:
- What is the relationship of the hierarchy to the laity? (CCCC qq. 177-193)
- Why do we need a hierarchy and a pope? (CCCC qq. 182-187)
- How does the Communion of Saints change the way I understand Jesus and His Church? (CCCC q: 194)
- How does the Communion of Saints influence the way I think about those who have died? (CCCC q: 195)

Blessed Virgin Mary:
- Why would Jesus leave Mary as Mother for all His family? (CCCC q: 196)
- How can one draw closer to Jesus by drawing closer to His Mother? (CCCC qq: 197, 199)
- How can a close relationship with Mary draw us into greater love for the Church? (CCCC q: 198)

NOTES:

TUTORIAL ON THE HIERARCHICAL STRUCTURE OF THE CHURCH

Head and Members: Hierarchy and authority:

The Church is not simply *like* a body, it is an organic unity in the Person of Jesus Christ in precisely the way a body is. We are so united that our works are united to His (Col 1:24); what happens to one member happens to all (1 Cor 12:26). We are radically united with Jesus Christ. If Christ is the Head and the Holy Spirit is the Soul, we might envision the visible hierarchy as the skeleton, which mediates the Head-Soul's upholding, guiding and directing the Body. Jesus' response to Peter's confession of faith suggests this way of viewing the Church's hierarchical structure (see Mt 16:16-19).

Peter alone is given the keys, yet it is Jesus' kingdom (see Jn 18:36). The meaning of Peter and the keys is linked to Jesus' identity as the Son of David (Mt 1:1), the Messiah King Who will lead David's new kingdom which will never end (Lk 1:32-33). The Church is the kingdom of heaven growing until it reaches its full maturity (Mk 4:30-32) and completion in heaven (1 Cor 15:24).

The kingdom is already on earth but the King must go to sit at the Father's right hand. Through the keys, Jesus indicates to the Apostles that in His absence, Peter is to rule His kingdom (see Is 22).

Here Isaiah prophesies to Shebna, the steward of King Hezekiah. Hezekiah is a king in the line of David. Shebna rules for Hezekiah with his authority, as father over David's household (i.e., kingdom) just as Hezekiah is father and king. However, Shebna is being replaced (Is 22:15-25). His replacement receives Hezekiah's keys and has the authority to open and shut all in the kingdom.

Peter's keys give him the authority "to bind and loose." In Jesus' time, binding and loosing became the Rabbis' divinely given authority to teach, govern and sanctify God's people. Peter, the Apostles and their successors have this same authority to bind and loose, but only Peter has the keys. In other words, only the pope has supreme authority over the universal Church.

Jesus reveals God does give such authority to men (Mt 23:2-3). He calls this authority Moses' chair (*cathedra*). The Lord of Lords, God Himself, tells *His* disciples while He is still with them that the Scribes and Pharisees have Moses's seat so the disciples must obey them. Jesus' own disciples must obey those whom He calls fools, blind guides and hypocrites while they have Moses' chair.

A Summary of the Teachings on the Blessed Virgin Mary (BVM)

Annunciation: The announcement to Mary by the Archangel Gabriel that she was chosen to bear God's Son (Lk. 1:26-38; CCC 484 - 489).

Apparitions: The appearance of the Blessed Virgin Mary (BVM) to someone on earth. Since all public Revelation ended with the last Apostle, it is at best private revelation and is only binding on the person receiving the revelation. There are many claims of apparitions, but only a few have been approved by the Church; a few of the approved apparitions include the Virgin of Guadalupe (1531), Immaculate Conception – Lourdes (1858), Our Lady of Knock (1879) and Our Lady of Fatima (1917). The Church does not require belief when she approves an apparition, but says that the apparition "is worthy of belief."

Assumption: The Fourth Marian Dogma which proclaims that Our Mother, at the end of her earthly life (called her "dormition" which means sleeping; the Church does not teach whether she died or not) was taken up bodily into heaven without the corruption of her body (CCC 966, cf. Rev. 12:1-2).

Christian Example of Obedience: Mary's complete submission to the will of God (cf. Lk. 1:38) is the model and example that each and every Christian is to strive for (CCC 144, 494, 511).

Devotions: Because of the BVM's special place in God's plan of salvation, she was the one to most totally participate with her Son's Redemptive life. She is to be honored in the same way that Jesus must honor her in His obedience to the 4th Commandment. This devotion is shown in many different ways in different cultures, such as venerating apparition sites and, through special names, prayers, Solemnities, Feasts and Memorials, etc. (CCC 971).

Fatima: A town in Portugal where the BVM appeared to three young children in 1916-1917. Central to Our Mother's message was prayer and repentance for the sins of the world. A miracle occurred on Oct 13, 1917 in which thousands experienced the sun "dancing" outside its normal track across the sky.

Fifth Marian "Dogma": A proposal from the faithful that the Church proclaim as dogma the roles of the BVM as Co-Redemptrix, Mediatrix of all Graces, and Advocate. The title Co-Redemptrix acknowledges the unique role the BVM had in God's plan of salvation - it DOES NOT make her equal with Jesus. Mediatrix of all Graces says that as Mother of the Church, Jesus has made Mary the medium through which God's grace is applied to the faithful. Advocate says that the BVM never stops pleading to her Son on behalf of the faithful. The Church has taught these consistently for 2000 years, but this is not yet considered a dogmatic teaching (CCC 964-965, 967 - 970).

Full of Grace: The term used by the angel Gabriel in Lk. 1:28 based on the Greek term *kecharitomine*. St. Jerome translated this as "full of grace" indicating that the BVM is perfected in grace; that is, made holy and perfected in love. This corresponds with the teachings that she did not have original sin (Immaculate Conception); that her body never corrupted and that she was taken up immediately into heaven at the end of her time on earth (Assumption). St. Joseph, husband of the BVM, would have had tremendous respect for her inexpressible sanctity for the sake of bearing the Son of God and would have understood that her natural motherhood was reserved for Jesus alone (Perpetual Virginity) (CCC 491, 508).

Hyperdulia: A Latin term, which is used to denote the highest "veneration" or honor that can paid to creatures; this hyperdulia is given only to the BVM as the Mother of God. *Dulia* is the honor we pay to the angels and saints. The "adoration" which we give to God alone is called *latria* in Latin.

Immaculate Conception: The Third Marian Dogma which proclaims that Our Blessed Mother was saved by Christ from the stain of original sin before her conception. This was accomplished by the Holy Spirit in anticipation of Jesus' Redemption of man on the Cross; something possible for God who transcends time (CCC 490 - 493).

Immaculate Heart: A devotion paid to the BVM begun in 1646 by St. John Eudes to inspire devotion to the Heart of Mary. Now celebrated as a Feast on the first Saturday following the second Sunday after Pentecost.

Lourdes: A town in France where our Blessed Mother appeared to St. Bernadette in 1858. Today pilgrims to Lourdes experience miraculous healings in the waters from the Grotto near which Mary appeared. In fact, a medical institute has been set up to document and study the large numbers of healings which come every year at Lourdes. Her appearance is celebrated on September 12th.

Magnificat: After Elizabeth proclaims Mary as "The Mother of my Lord," Mary responds to Elizabeth that Mary's soul "magnifies" the Lord. Mary affirms in her Magnificat the great gifts God has bestowed upon her and on mankind (Lk. 1:46-55).

Mother of the Church: The Church is the Mystical Body of Christ (see Eph. 5:23) and we are members of Christ's Body (1 Cor. 12:27); therefore, Mary is Our Mother which St. John affirms for us in Revelation 12:17 (CCC 502-507, 963-965).

Mother of God: See *Theotokos*

New Eve: Eve prefigured Mary. The early Church Fathers saw that just as Eve was the mother of a fallen human race, Mary is the mother and the cooperating cause of the redeemed human race (CCC 721-726).

Perpetual Virginity: The Second Marian Dogma declares that Mary was a virgin when she bore Jesus, and remained a virgin throughout her life (CCC 496 - 50, 510). There are three principle objections to her perpetual virginity. Scripture says Jesus has brothers and sisters, that Mary and Joseph had no relations "until" Jesus was born, and that Jesus is the firstborn Son. First, let us look at the issue of *"brothers and sisters."*

Brothers and Sisters: Mt. 13:55 and Mk. 6:3 name the following as brothers of Jesus: James, Joseph (sometimes Joses - the manuscripts vary on the spelling), Simon and Judas, but Mt. 27:56 says at the cross that a Mary present is the mother of James and Joseph but this cannot be the BVM or they would refer to her as Jesus' Mother as well; Mk. 15:40 says Mary the mother of James the younger and Joses was there. Jn. 19:25 says that Mary His Mother, the BVM's sister, Mary the wife of Clopas, and Mary Magdalene were there. Hebrew and Aramaic *ah* was used for various types of relations: brother, blood-relation, companion, fellow tribesman, country man, etc. Hebrew had no word for cousin. The tradition of using "brother" for all family relations was kept in the Greek Old Testament and continued to be followed in the Greek New Testament and this is obviously being used in these references to Jesus' brothers.

Until: Most ancient words have a broad span of possible meanings. Sometimes the Greek word for "until" leaves room for a change after the point in time indicated. However, not always. In Dt. 34:6 Moses was buried and "until this day no one knows where the grave is." That was true in the day of the writer of Dt. and it is still true even today. In Mt. 28:20 Jesus promised to be with His Church, His followers, "until" the end of the world; nor will He desert us in eternity.

Firstborn: Jesus is called Firstborn in Lk. 2:7 (and also in Mt. 1:25 if we take the Vulgate addition to the Greek). This reflects the Hebrew word *bekor*, which means the privileged position of the firstborn under Jewish law, who would inherit a double portion of all that belonged to his father, as well as inheriting his name and position as patriarch of the family. It is a legal title and need not imply there were other children.

Rosary: A devotional prayer which meditates on 20 mysteries which comprise major events in Jesus' life. It is comprised of a series of one "Our Father" and 10 "Hail Mary" prayers that one prays while meditating on one of the mysteries. The mysteries are divided into 4 sets of five mysteries: The Joyful, Sorrowful, Glorious and Luminous mysteries. Traditionally one set of five mysteries is prayed on a specific day: Glorious-Sun/Wed, Joyful-Mon/Sat, Sorrowful-Tues/Fri, Luminous-Thurs (CCC 971, 2678, 2708). See page 114 for more details on praying the Rosary.

Theotokos: This was the First Marian Dogma to be proclaimed in the very early years of the Church (CCC 495, 509). *Theotokos* is Greek for "God Bearer," emphasizing that Mary is not only the Mother of Jesus, but since Jesus is truly man and truly God she is also properly called the Mother of God.

THE CATHOLIC FAITH AT A GLANCE: A SUMMARY

God:

The model (page 82) begins with God at the top, revealing that He is a Trinity of Persons. God is a Communion of total self-giving love. The circle reflects that God is one nature of unchanging, active, infinite, absolute perfection. It also reflects that this one, absolutely perfect nature is fully possessed by three infinite Persons.

The three Persons give and receive themselves eternally and without change. God is love; divine love is an eternal total Self-giving and receiving among the divine Persons. God's love begins with the Father who gives Himself totally, in His Eternal Word, the Son. The Son receives Himself and all He is, and in love and thanksgiving He returns Himself to the Father. The Holy Spirit is the fruit of the Father's and Son's love. In God, Love is fruitful; it is life-giving; it is a divine Person.

The First Creation:

Everything in the circle is God and cannot change, and so God's eternal love cannot change. God's love is the pattern for all other authentic love. God exists necessarily but He has the ability to share this eternal love and so He chooses to create in order to do so. He creates angels and all visible creation first, and then He creates man. There is an infinite difference between God and creation but also great similarity. God is infinite and unchangeable; creation is finite and changing. Yet all of creation still necessarily reflects its divine archetype. It mirrors the Trinitarian pattern and so it must receive itself and in thanksgiving, return itself to God. The solid line represents the fact that man and all of creation are initially in communion with God. The dashed line represents the task of man's return of himself to God after the pattern of the Son.

The Fall of Man:

Our first parents, on behalf of all creation, were to receive themselves in thanksgiving and return themselves to God but they refused thereby rupturing communion between God and His creation, leaving this first creation broken.

The New Creation:

God is communion itself and so He will not leave His creation separated from Him. However, the problem is man's action has left an infinite breach between God and creation. Man must return himself to God but we need an infinite Man to overcome the infinite gap. This is the reason for the Incarnation in which the Son of God joins Himself so radically to a human nature, it belongs to Him. We call this the Incarnation, "the Word becomes flesh and dwells among us" (Jn. 1:14).

Jesus Christ now does what Adam and Eve refused to do. He receives His human life and in love—on the Cross, history's greatest act of love—and thanksgiving, returns it to the Father for our sake, thereby reconciling humanity and all creation with God in Himself.

Lost communion remains for everyone, who is born as a child of Adam and Eve, born into a "relational dead end." Each person can "return" to communion with God only by being united with Christ.

This is the reason for Sacraments. We must follow the path Jesus gave us. We must go through the Cross to die to the fallen, first creation and rise again with Him in the new creation of His Body, the Church. Union with Christ is union with the Catholic Church. Death and rebirth are through the Sacrament of Baptism.

The rest of Jesus Christ's Good News, the entirety of the Catholic faith, can be understood in terms of this communion model. God is Communion, creation is a gift of communion, communion is lost in the Fall, and communion is restored through Jesus Christ. The opportunity for man to be incorporated into this beautiful drama of communion is through the Catholic Church and by cooperating with these gifts Christ left for us.

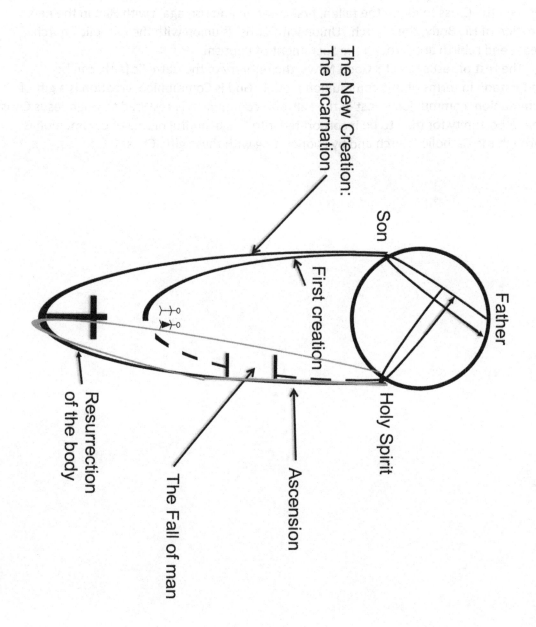

The New Creation:
The Incarnation

Son

Father

First creation

Holy Spirit

Resurrection
of the body

The Fall of man

Ascension

NOTES

SESSION 8: SIN, GRACE, JUSTIFICATION & THE SACRAMENTAL SYSTEM

READING ASSIGNMENT

Page 56: questions 200-201; pages 65-70: questions 218-232; pages 114-115: questions 391-400; pages 121-122: questions 422-428

STUDY QUESTIONS

Sin:
- What is sin? (CCCC q: 392)
- What does sin mean for your relationship with God and others? (CCCC q: 391)
- What does sin mean for your personal fulfillment? (CCCC qq: 359-362, 393-399)

Grace & Justification:
- What is grace? (CCCC qq: 231, 422-425)
- Why is grace necessary for happiness on earth and eternally?
  (CCCC qq: 228-230, 232)
- What does it mean to cooperate with grace? (CCCC qq: 378-388)
- What does it mean to be justified? (CCCC qq: 131, 263, 422)
- How does justification relate to my search for happiness? (CCCC qq: 425, 428)

The Sacramental System:
- How does conforming my life to the liturgical life aid in achieving happiness?
  (CCCC qq: 218-223, 241-242)
- What is a Sacrament? (CCCC qq: 224-228, 250)
- How do Sacraments correspond to my desire for happiness? (CCCC qq: 229-232)

NOTES:

Fr. Robert Barron – 7 Deadly Sins & 7 Lively Virtues

Seven Deadly Sins	Lively Virtues (antidote)	Marian Example
Fear – the Source of All Sin	Jesus raises Lazarus from the dead – unbinds him – he recovers and is released from sin	
1. **PRIDE** – False self-view, the root of all sin Lucifer Adam/Eve Us	**HUMILITY** – the truth of who we are All is God's – we are simply stewards	Annunciation – Let it be done to me according to thy word (Luke 1:38)
2. **AVARICE** – Unreasonable desire for riches Prevents you from seeing the common good We must use our property for common good Prodigal Son is example of avarice	**GENEROSITY** – giving with God's generosity Father to Son & Holy Spirit – divine generosity God's generous love seen in creation Are we cheerful givers?	Birth of Jesus – Giving birth in a stable amidst poverty (Luke 2:7)
3. **ENVY** – Desire destruction of goods we can't have Sorry at another's good (Pleasure at another's sorrow) Envy tends to scapegoat; blame someone else	**ADMIRATION** – recognizing all gifts from God Go out of your way to praise someone else	Wedding Feast at Cana "They have no wine" (John 2:3) "Do whatever He tells you" (Jn 2:5)
4. **WRATH** – Desire for revenge Family members not talking for years/decades - getting back Smoke blinds and chokes (Gethsemane Peter cuts off the ear we don't listen)	**FORGIVENESS** – loving with merciful love Central to Jesus's message Active engagement of evil Stand your ground, but in love Write a note to someone forgiving him	Finding in the Temple Say only the good things people need to hear. "We have been looking for you" (Luke 2:48)
5. **LUST** – Treating another human as a means to satisfy sexual desire Spouses mustn't lust after each other	**CHASTITY** Sexual uprightness Respect for the other as other -- Refuse to misuse Pornography a great threat to chastity	Annunciation – "I do not know man" Mary's Perpetual Virginity (Lk 1:34)
6. **GLUTTONY** – Immoderate pleasure in food or drink Our hearts are restless until they rest in Thee	**ASCETICISM** – abstaining from goods Instead of eating, pray! Fast; skip a meal – spend prayer and $$ to poor Leave the table a little hungry	Open my lips – proclaim Thy praise
7. **SLOTH** – Boredom, inactivity @ spiritual level Sorrow in regards to spiritual goods Indifferent – can't care less – spiritual "relativism"	**ZEAL** – excitement/drive for the mission Ask God for your mission, purpose in life Corporal & spiritual works of mercy Mass – Source & Summit – 70% of Catholics don't attend Mass; all Christians are sent	The Visitation Mary proceeded in haste to see Elizabeth (Luke 1:39)

GRACE AND JUSTIFICATION DEFINITIONS

Actual Grace: God's interventions, given before an action, moving one to conversion or moving one toward acceptance of God's will in the work of sanctification (CCC 2000).

Ex opere operato: The Latin which means, "by the very fact of the action being performed," referring to the way that the seven Sacraments work. By the very fact they are performed, Gods' grace is given but the fruitfulness depends upon the disposition of the person receiving the Sacrament, regardless of the holiness of the minister (CCC 1128).

Fruitfulness: The amount of benefit or supernatural transformation (becoming perfected in love), achieved in a person receiving God's grace.

Good Works: Man's free response to God's grace given to increase in a life of holiness and required for the process of Justification. These works include keeping God's commands, acts of faith, hope and charity, as well as prayer and self-mortification (CCC 2012-2016).

Grace: The favor, free and undeserved help that God gives and we must respond to by accepting or rejecting. Grace is a supernatural participation in God's life where we become partakers of the divine nature (see 2 Peter 1:4) and achieve the intimacy of the Trinitarian life (CCC 1996-2005).

Habitual Grace: Grace which gives us the permanent disposition to live and act as God calls us to; totally submitting ourselves to His will. It is roughly the same as sanctifying grace (CCC 2000).

Holiness: The degree to which we become sanctified, primarily achieved through response to habitual grace (CCC 2012-2016).

Justification: The <u>process</u> by which a sinner is made righteous, pure and holy (sanctified) before God by accepting God's righteousness through faith in Jesus Christ, conferred through Baptism. Justification has been merited for us by Jesus' Passion, Death and Resurrection. It makes possible our free cooperation with God's grace. Justification, <u>a process</u>, can be lost and regained (CCC 1987-1995).

Merit: Attributing to man, the reward due for good works done in a disposition of charity, but primarily attributed to God who has called man to good works through His grace (CCC 2006-2011).

Righteousness: The state of justice before God whereby we can receive grace. Very closely associated, if not synonymous with Justification (CCC 1991).

Sacramental Grace: The gifts proper to each individual Sacrament (CCC 2003).

Salvation: Eternal happiness in God's presence if one dies in a state of Justification (CCC 1992).

Sanctification: The entire <u>process</u> whereby a person is supernaturally transformed, chiefly by cooperating with habitual grace, and is perfected in a life of Christian love/charity (CCC 1999 - 2001).

Sanctifying Grace: The gift of God's own life infused in us by the Holy Spirit, to heal us of the spiritual damage we cause to ourselves by our sins, and to sanctify us. It is a stable, supernatural disposition which perfects the soul so it can live and act in God's love (CCC 1999-2000).

Special Grace: Referred to as charisms (from the Greek for gifts) which help to make sanctifying grace fruitful in us and are intended for the common good of the entire Church (CCC 2003).

TUTORIAL ON THE RELATIONSHIP BETWEEN THE LITURGY AND SALVATION HISTORY

The Liturgical Arc

We have shown God is a Communion of Persons Who share their overflowing love by creating angels and man. Some angels rebelled and since angelic persons can't change they can't repent, so fallen angels are forever damned. However, man also rebelled, rupturing his communion with God. But he can repent and be restored to communion. In order for man to be restored to communion, he must be able to love infinitely. Only union with God makes such love possible. The Son became Man to restore communion by conforming His human will to His divine will in a life of total Self-gift.

Each person now has access to Jesus' gift of love by dying to the fallen, first creation and rising to new life in Christ. This new life is a new creation; the Church (2 Cor 5:17). It's the only pathway to new life because it's the image of Trinitarian love. The Son's love enters time in the Incarnation, and shows its fullness in Jesus' Passion, Resurrection and Pentecost. We call this path, which the Church continues to make present throughout the lives of her members, the liturgy.

The Liturgy, the Trinity and Salvation History:

The profound meaning of the liturgy is revealed through creation's and salvation history's reflection of their Trinitarian archetype (see sessions 3 & 5). The Son's begetting and the Holy Spirit's spiration are not only the archetypes for creation and redemption, they are also the archetypes of the liturgy.

The begetting of the Son and His eternal return to the Father is the eternal action of Eucharist. The Son eternally empties Himself in thanksgiving (Greek: *eucharistia*) and returns Himself in love, forming the pattern of the created order, of salvation history, as well as of the liturgy and the life of each Christian. The liturgy makes present to every Christian and to the Church throughout time, what the Son does eternally and what He did on the Cross. From this love's bursting into time, the Holy Spirit pours forth at Pentecost upon a fallen creation and into the Church, the Body of Christ.

Sacraments of Initiation and the Trinity:

As the liturgy reflects the interior life of the Trinity and salvation history, so do the Sacraments of Initiation. Baptism initiates each Christian into this eternal relationship and historical drama. It is the Sacrament corresponding to the Son's begetting and to His Incarnation.

The relationship by which the Holy Spirit proceeds as the Love and the Communion of the Father and the Son is made present in Salvation History at Pentecost. Each Christian is initiated into this relationship in Confirmation, sometimes called the Sacrament of Pentecost. Thus, we say Confirmation perfects baptismal grace.

The final Sacrament of Initiation is the Eucharist. It is the repeatable consummation of our communion with Christ and the Trinity.

The Mass: The Sacrifice of Love:

The Son's eternal thanksgiving, His Passion, Death and Resurrection, and the Eucharist are intertwined acts of love. All three are the same infinite act of the Son: the first in eternity, the second in history and the third in the present. The Mass makes present the Incarnate Son's act of total Self-giving love each time it is celebrated. It is the liturgical fullness of Christ's sacrificial love and so it's called the Sacrifice of the Mass. It unites the participants in the Son's love and into the life of the Trinity, brought about through the power of the Holy Spirit and mediated by the actions of the priest. It's the most sublime encounter with Jesus Christ possible on earth.

Interior Life of the Trinity	Salvation History	Liturgy/ Sacramental System
Begetting of the Son	Incarnation to Ascension	Baptism
Spiration of the Holy Spirit	Pentecost	Confirmation
Eternal Communion	Life of the Church throughout history	Eucharist

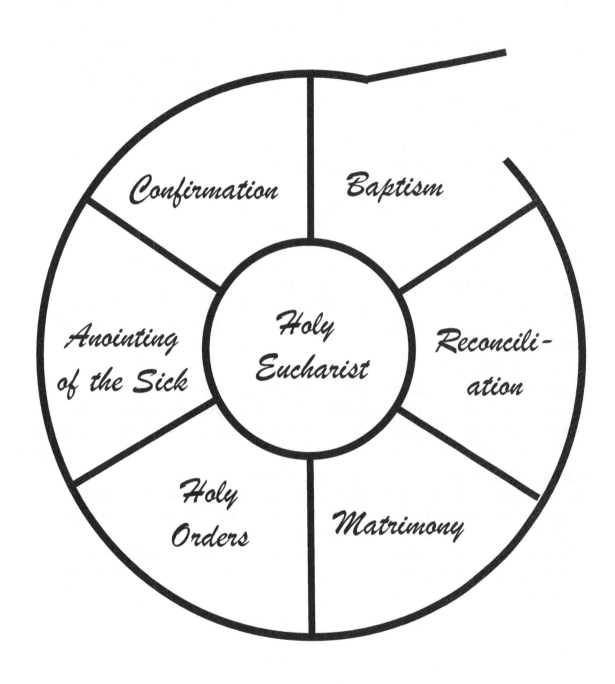

THE SACRAMENTS AT A GLANCE

The Sacraments are signs of God's love using events in Salvation History. At the same time, they are intimate, personal encounters of communion with Jesus Christ and so they mediate His saving power (also called grace). Through the Sacraments you enter into a real communion with Christ, partake in His divine nature, and are transformed by His powerful love. Through the Sacraments you are given the power to help proclaim and build God's kingdom on earth and strengthen the unity of God's People.

Sacraments of Initiation
1. *Baptism*: You die to your fallen self and are raised a new creation in the Resurrection of Jesus Christ, thereby you are freed from sin, given a new life of grace in the Holy Spirit, and become a member of the Body of Christ, the Catholic Church.
2. *Confirmation*: The completion of baptismal grace is a gift of the Holy Spirit that further strengthens you to live and to proclaim the Gospel, to serve others and to defend the faith.
3. Holy *Eucharist*: The Passion, Death and Resurrection are made present in the Mass. In the Eucharistic Prayer, the bread and wine are really and truly "transubstantiated" into the Body, Blood, Soul and Divinity of Our Lord Jesus Christ. In Holy Communion we enter into an unspeakable, one flesh union with Him through receiving His Body and Blood.

Sacraments of Healing
4. *Reconciliation*: Jesus Christ forgives our sins through the person of His priest.
5. *Anointing of the Sick*: A priest anoints with sacred oil a person who is sick or for whom death is a possibility, which brings about a healing of the soul (and sometimes the body) through the forgiveness of sins.

Sacraments in the Service of Communion and Mission
6. *Matrimony*: A man and a woman enter into a life-long covenant of love, made supernaturally effective by Christ's Cross. Through marriage, they serve each other, their children and the Church in God's plan of salvation.
7. *Holy Orders*: Jesus Christ ordains men (males) through His Holy Spirit as deacons, priests, and bishops to teach, govern, and sanctify His Church in His Person, with His authority and His divine power.

SACRAMENTS SUMMARY CHART

Prepared by Steve Ray

The Seven Sacraments of the Church

Sacrament	Minister	Scripture	Required State	Frequency	Effect	Form	Matter
Baptism CCC 1213-1284	Ordinary: a Bishop, priest or deacon; Extraordinary: any person if necessary (CCC 1256)	Mt 28:19-20; Jn 3:5; 4:1-2; Acts 2:38; 22:16; Rom 6:3-4; Mk 16:16; Titus 3:5; Eph 5:26; 1 Peter 3:21	Unbaptized pagan, convert to the Christian Faith, newborn infant (CCC 1246-1255)	Only applied once (Eph 4:5; CCC 1272)	Removes Original and Actual sin (CCC 1263); causes New Birth ("born again") (CCC 1265); incorporates into Christ (CCC 1267); is the doorway into the Church (CCC 846, 1213)	"I baptize you in the Name of the Father, and of the Son, and of the Holy Spirit." Mt 28:18-19; CCC 1240)	Water (Immersion, Infusion, or Sprinkling) (CCC 1278)
Confirmation CCC 1285-1321	Ordinary: the Bishop. Extraordinary: a Priest (CCC 1313, 1318)	Acts 8:14-17; 9:17-19; 19:6; Heb 6:1-6	Baptized but unconfirmed; needed Completion of Baptismal grace (CCC 1285); Baptized Christians from other traditions incorporated into the fullness of the Catholic Church	Only applied once (CCC 1304)	Sign of consecration (CCC 1294); spiritual seal (CCC 1293); completion of baptismal grace (CCC 1285); full outpouring of the Holy Spirit (CCC 1302-1303)	"Be sealed with the Gift of the Holy Spirit." (CCC 1300)	Holy Chrism (Blessed Oil) and the Laying on of hands by the Bishop or a delegated priest (CCC 1288, 1294, 1300)
Eucharist CCC 1322-1421	The Priest (CCC 1411)	Jn 6:1-71; Mt 26:26-28; Mk 14:22-25; Lk 22:7-20; 24:13-53; Acts 2:42-47; 20:7; 1 Cor 10:16-21	All Catholics are encouraged to participate (CCC 1417); Baptized believers in Communion with the Catholic Church (CCC 1396-1401) and devoid of Mortal Sin (CCC 1415)	Minimum of once a year, as frequently as daily (CCC 1389; 1417)	Intimate union with Christ (CCC 1391); Receiving Christ; nourish spiritual life; medicine of immortality, separating us from sin, removal of venial sin, spiritual strength, unites the Body into One (CCC 1391-1401)	"This My Body which will be given up for you. Do this in memory of Me. ... Take this, all of you, and drink from it: this is the cup of my Blood, the Blood of the New and Everlasting Covenant. It will be shed for you and for all so that sins may be forgiven. Do this in memory of me." (CCC 1412; 1 Cor 11:24-25)	Bread and Wine (CCC 1333)

Sacrament	Minister	Scripture	Required State	Frequency	Effect	Form	Matter
Confession, Penance or Reconciliation CCC 1422-1498	The Priest (CCC 1461)	Jn 20:23; Mt 16:18-19; 18:15-18; James 5:14-15	In Mortal Sin; desiring the Grace of Confession; in need of spiritual guidance (CCC 1446)	Minimum of once a year, or as frequently as necessary (CCC 1457-1458)	Forgiveness of serious sin, reunification with the Church, reconciled the Spirit, cleansing of conscience, restores grace (CCC 1468-1470)	"God, the Father of mercies, through the death and resurrection of his Son has reconciled the world to himself and sent the Holy Spirit among us for the forgiveness of sins; through the ministry of the Church, may God give you pardon and peace, and I absolve you from your sins in the name of the Father, and of the Son, and of the Holy Spirit." (CCC 1449)	Sins; Contrition and confession; priestly words of absolution (CCC 1480)
Marriage CCC 1601-1666	The Spouses, with the priest or deacon as witness (CCC 1623)	Gen 1:27-28; 2:18-25; Mt 19:3-12; Jn 2:1-11; Eph 5:25-32;	Each spouse must be a baptized man and woman with no impediment to marriage (CCC 1625)	Once and to one spouse as long as the spouse is living; again only if the spouse dies (CCC 2382)	The two become one flesh (Eph 5:31; perpetual and exclusive covenant partners (CCC 1638-1640)	The "I do", by which both spouses indicate their mutual consent to the marriage covenant (CCC 1626-1628)	Mutual Consent and Covenant to live together as husband and wife (CCC 1626); and the consummation of the Marriage (CCC 1640)
Holy Orders CCC 1536-1600	The Bishop (CCC 1576)	Acts 6:5-6; 13:3; 14:23; 20:21-23; Jn 20:21-23; 1 Tim 3:1; 4:14; 2 Tim 1:6; Titus 1:5; Phil 1:1	A Baptized man who has been called for ordination by God; in the Western rite, with the exception of permanent deacons, the ordained must be celibate (CCC 1577-1580)	Only once; separate ordination for Deacon, Priest, and Bishop (CCC 1582)	A special relationship to Christ to lead and serve the Church; indelible spiritual character imprinted on the soul (CCC 1581; 1594)	The Bishop's "specific consecratory prayer asking God for the outpouring of the Holy Spirit and his gifts proper to the ministry to which the candidate is being ordained" (CCC 1573)	Laying on of the Bishop's hands with the consecratory prayer (CCC 1538)
Anointing of the Sick, Extreme Unction, and Last Rites CCC 1499-1535	Only a Bishop or Priest (CCC 1516)	Mk 6:13; Jn 20:23; Mt 16:18-19; 18:15-18; James 5:14-15	Seriously ill; at the point of death or before a serious operation or for the elderly whose frailty becomes more pronounced (CCC 1541f.)	Repeatable; at the point of grave illnesses or before a serious operation (CCC 1514f.)	Sins forgiven; grace to face trial; spiritual preparation to die; and if God's will, physical healing (CCC 1520-1523)	Prayer of the Priest over the sick person for the grace of the Holy Spirit and the forgiveness of sins (CCC 1513, 1519)	Anointing with Holy Oil and Imposition of Hands (CCC 1513, 1519)

NOTES

NOTES

SESSION 9: THE LITURGY, THE LITURGICAL YEAR & THE MASS

READING ASSIGNMENT

Pages 67-74: questions 221-249; pages 99-100: questions 351-356

STUDY QUESTIONS

Liturgy:
- What is the purpose of the liturgy? (CCCC qq: 218-219)
- What is the relationship between the earthly liturgy and the heavenly liturgy? (CCCC qq: 233-235)

The Liturgical Year:
- What is the purpose of the liturgical year? (CCCC q: 242)
- What is the center of the liturgical year and why? (CCCC q: 241)

Mass:
- What is the relationship between sacrifice and love? (CCCC qq: 271, 274, 280, 281)
- How does the holiness of the Mass relate to my holiness? (CCCC qq: 281, 291, 292, 294)
- How does the Mass correspond to the events of Calvary, Easter Sunday, Pentecost, and to eternity in heaven? (CCCC qq: 276, 280, 281, 282, 287, 288, 294)
- How does my participation in Mass affect my life? (CCCC qq: 281, 282, 289, 292, 294)
- How does the Mass correspond to my vocation and my longing for infinite love and eternal life? (CCCC qq. 281, 282, 294)

NOTES:

LITURGY IN THE LIFE OF THE CHURCH (CCC 1076-1112; 1135-1209; 1667-1690)

Liturgy

The term originally comes from the Greek word, *leitourgia*, which meant "work of the people," or "public works." In the Church, it means public worship most perfectly celebrated in The Holy Sacrifice of the Mass. The term "liturgy" is usually used to mean the Mass; it can also refer to other forms of public worship officially designated by the Church as explained below under Other Liturgical Celebrations.

Liturgical Rites:

The liturgy is the universal action of the Church by which Christians throughout time participate in the one Sacrifice of the Cross. The liturgy unites all Christians, with Christ and one another, in the truth of worship given to us directly by Our Lord at the Last Supper. But while every liturgy has the same source (Jesus Christ), the same meaning, and the same basic form, it also has a variety of expressions. We call these different expressions, Rites.

The Rites are most generally divided between the Western Rites and the Eastern Rites. Within the Western or Latin Rites, the primary form is the Roman Rite. The most common form of the Roman Rite in use today is called the Ordinary Form. This came into use in the early 1970s, but the previous form in use since the 16th century is also still celebrated and is referred to as the Extraordinary Form. However, there are also several other forms of the Roman Rite, all approved by the Church.

The form of the Mass used in the Personal Ordinariates (of which Our Lady of the Atonement is a member) is called Divine Worship (formerly called the Book of Divine Worship and colloquially referred to as the "Anglican Use Mass" or even the "Anglican Use Rite"). The Roman Rite also has other special forms, though now rarely used, such as the Zaire Use, the Algonquian Use and the Iroquoian Use. In the Latin Rite, there are also other Rites not under the Roman Rite, such as the Ambrosian Rite, the Mozarabic Rite, the Carthusian Rite, the Rite of Braga, and the Benedictine Rite.

The Eastern Rites also have a variety of Rites used by many Eastern Catholic churches. The most prevalent is the Byzantine Rite celebrated by fourteen different Eastern Catholic churches. There are also the Alexandrian Rite, the Armenian Rite, the East Syrian Rite and the West Syrian Rite.

Liturgical seasons:

Every liturgical rite celebrates Jesus' saving work throughout each year by commemorating the most significant events in the plan of salvation. The two major events around which the entire liturgical calendar is formed, are those associated with Jesus' birth and His manifestation to the world. In addition to these major events, we also celebrate other significant events in salvation history and we also recall the lives of

Christians who were exceptional witnesses to Christ who we call saints. The celebration of each saint is often on the day he entered into eternal life. The various rites celebrate the events according to slightly different names, but the most common names for two major events from salvation history are Christmas, Lent, Holy Week, and Easter. Each week is also celebrated as a mini-liturgical year with Friday celebrating the Passion and Sunday commemorating Easter. We will discuss the liturgical calendar more in the following section on the Liturgical Year.

The Sacred Liturgy or **The Holy Sacrifice of the Mass**:
Pope John Paul II says, "The Eucharist is above all else a sacrifice. It is the sacrifice of the Redemption and also the sacrifice of the New Covenant..." This is the most holy prayer the Church can offer because it offers back to the Father, the Sacrifice His Son offered on our behalf. This is the summit of Christian liturgy. Therefore, in the West we often refer to this sacred liturgy as The Holy Sacrifice of the Mass.

Other Liturgical Celebrations:
Rites of the Sacraments: The Celebration of the seven Sacraments is part of the Church's public worship. In fact, all of the Sacraments can be celebrated as part of the Sacred Liturgy, but if not they are still considered public worship offered by the Church.

Good Friday: The Friday of Holy Week is the only day of the year when Mass is not celebrated. Good Friday liturgy includes the Liturgy of the Word concluding with the Passion of the Lord from the Gospel of St. John, followed by Veneration of the Cross and concluding with Holy Communion, which was consecrated on Holy Thursday.

Daily Office or Liturgy of the Hours (Divine Office): The official public prayer of the Church is called the Daily Office in Divine Worship and the Liturgy of the Hours in the Ordinary Form. It is comprised of hymns, the Psalms, other Scripture readings, and writings of the Saints or other spiritual readings. It is usually said in public at different hours of the day. In Divine Worship, there are four times: Morning Prayer, Noontime Prayer, Evening Prayer, and Compline (the prayer said before retiring).

The Ordinary Form has additional hours. It also has Morning prayer and Evening Prayer which are referred to as the hinge hours because the whole cycle of daily prayers depends upon them. Midday prayer is comprised of Midmorning prayer, Midday prayer and Mid-afternoon prayer. While some contemplative communities are required to say all three midday prayers, for most it suffices to say only one. Night Prayer is said before retiring even if it is after midnight. Finally, the Office of Readings can be said anytime, but in contemplative communities it must be said in the morning.

The offices in the Extraordinary Form are called Matins (Office of Readings), Lauds (Morning Prayer), Prime, Terce, Sext, None (these four times are Midday Prayers; all were usually said), Vespers (Evening Prayer), and Compline (Night Prayer).

The Divine Office is usually chanted in choir in contemplative communities. It is a requirement for clergy and religious. It is optional but highly encouraged for the laity. For laity who cannot keep the entire day, Morning Prayer, Evening Prayer (and in the Ordinary Form, the Office of Readings) are recommended.

Benediction of the Blessed Sacrament (Adoration of the Blessed Sacrament): In this devotion the Blessed Sacrament is placed in the monstrance, which is put on the altar with at least two lighted candles, and then the Blessed Sacrament is incensed. Hymns (customary are *Pange lingua, Tantum ergo* and *O salutaris Hostia*) are sung and Scripture readings are read. This devotion is performed by a bishop, priest or deacon. For prolonged adoration, the Blessed Sacrament may be left exposed (while it is exposed, someone *must* always be present), during which time those present pray in silence.

The Christian Funeral: This is part of the public celebration of the Church, but it is not a Sacrament or Sacramental because the deceased is beyond the sacramental economy. However, if done as part of the Mass, grace may be applied to reduce time the deceased may spend in Purgatory. The Rite expresses the communion the Church on earth has with the deceased.

Sacramentals: Are signs instituted by the Church that do not confer grace in the way that Sacraments do, but they prepare us to receive grace and dispose us to cooperate with it. They always include prayer and usually are accompanied by a sign such as the sprinkling of holy water, the sign of the cross, or laying on of hands. Most Sacramentals are extensions of the Sacraments. First place among Sacramentals are blessings (e.g., of articles, meals, places and people). Consecrations are blessings with lasting importance which reserve objects to liturgical use and people to a life of dedicated service to God (e.g., of virgins). Exorcisms are ceremonies in which the Church asks authoritatively, in the name of Jesus Christ, that a person or object be protected from the power of the evil one.

Popular Devotions:

These are not strictly liturgical in character, but are closely connected with the liturgy. They have been supported and encouraged by the Church. They extend and support the liturgical life of the Church, but do not replace it.

Angelus: A devotion in honor of the Incarnation using the Hail Mary and commemorating the Annunciation. The Angelus is recited three times daily, at 6am, noon and 6pm, traditionally while a bell is rung.

Chaplet of the Divine Mercy: A prayer privately revealed in a vision by Jesus to St. Faustina. This Chaplet offers back to God, the Body, Blood, Soul and Divinity of Our Lord Jesus Christ as restitution for our sins and the sins of the world. It is popularly sung, but can also be spoken and follows the pattern of the Rosary beginning with the Our Father, then the Hail Mary and Apostles Creed. Then on the large beads a prayer offering Jesus to the Father for atonement for sins and on the small beads a prayer asking for mercy on us for the sake of Jesus' Passion. This is repeated for 5 decades. See page 115 for a picture illustrating the use of the Rosary for the Chaplet of the Divine Mercy.

First Friday: Devotion rendered to the Sacred Heart of Jesus on the First Friday of nine consecutive months. The devotion is kept by receiving Communion on First Friday; a devotion which is usually kept year-round. This devotion was as a result of the private revelation to St. Margaret Mary Alacoque.

First Saturday: Devotion rendered to the Immaculate Heart of Mary on the First Saturday of the month for five consecutive months as a result of her private revelations at Fatima. The devotion is kept by going to confession, receiving Communion, reciting five decades of the Rosary and meditating on these Mysteries for 15 minutes. Many places also offer a Votive Mass on these Saturdays.

First Thursday: Christians are asked to receive Communion and pray for increased vocations to the priesthood and for continuing strength for every priest's active ministry on the first Thursday of each month in honor of Christ the Eternal High Priest.

Forty Hours: A devotion to honor the forty hours that the Body of Jesus spent in the tomb before His Resurrection on Easter Sunday. The Blessed Sacrament is solemnly exposed for these forty hours when the faithful adore Jesus in this Most Holy Sacrament. This devotion is usually begun and ended with a Mass, procession and the Litany of the Saints.

Lectio Divina: The reading of and meditation on Sacred Scripture focused on deepening one's understanding of the major themes of the Bible. It is performed as part of the Church's liturgical life.

Novenas: Any prayer said for nine consecutive days focusing on a special intention. The first novena (Novena to the Holy Spirit) was said by the Blessed Mother and Apostles in the upper room between the Ascension and Pentecost.

Pilgrimages: A trip to a Holy Place for the purpose of a specific intention or for spiritual growth.

Rosary: A devotional prayer which meditates on 20 mysteries which comprise major events in Jesus' life. The Rosary begins with the Apostle's Creed, one "Hour Father," three "Hail Mary," and one "Glory Be" prayers. This introductory set of prayers is followed by a series of one "Our Father," 10 "Hail Mary prayers," and one "Glory Be," and is usually completed with the Fatima prayer. A final series of prayers is said after repeating 5 mysteries. One meditates on one of 20 different mysteries while saying the above prayers. The mysteries are divided into 4 sets of five mysteries termed the Joyful,

Luminous, Sorrowful and Glorious mysteries. Traditionally, one mystery is prayed on a particular day: Glorious—Sun/Wed, Joyful—Mon/Sat, Luminous—Thurs, Sorrowful—Tues/Fri, (CCC 971, 2678, 2708). See page 114 for a Guide to Praying the Rosary.

Stations of the Cross: A devotion begun in the Middle Ages after the Muslim invasion of the Holy Land when pilgrims could no longer visit there safely. The Stations of the Cross are a series of 14 stations which represent Jesus' Passion as He suffered from the trial before Pilate, through Calvary and to the Tomb. At each station people stop, a prayer is said and a reflection is read.

Veneration of the Cross: Honoring Christ crucified by paying homage to His image on a Cross. This devotion is a liturgical act during Holy Friday's celebration where the faithful come forward to offer reverence to the Cross, usually by kneeling and kissing the Cross.

THE LITURGICAL YEAR

The liturgical year in every rite is organized around the celebration of 1) the Incarnation-Nativity-Manifestation of the Lord and 2) His Passion, Death and Resurrection. We also celebrate the lives of our Blessed Mother and the Saints (called the Sanctoral) throughout this annual cycle. The feasts are observed in three degrees of solemnity: Solemnities are the highest order, Feasts are the next, and Memorials (there are obligatory and optional memorials) are the lowest level of solemnity. An overview of the liturgical year for each of the four forms (Divine Worship, Ordinary Form, Extraordinary Form, and Byzantine Rite) can be found beginning on page 105.

Sanctoral Cycle: The annual cycle in which we celebrate Christ's mysteries includes the special veneration of the Blessed Virgin Mary, Mother of God. Her veneration is intimately and inseparably united with Her Son's work of salvation. She is the exemplar of Christian witness and irreplaceable in her role in God's place of salvation. The feast days of martyrs and other saints are also celebrated throughout the year on dates significant to that martyr or saint (often the day they died). In every celebration of a saint, as with the celebration of Our Blessed Mother, we are commemorating Christ's saving work on the Cross.

Stationary and Movable Feasts: Stationary feasts are those celebrated on specific dates in the civil calendar throughout the year. The stationary feasts include the Nativity, the Epiphany, and most days of the Sanctoral cycle. The movable feasts are those that are celebrated on different dates in the civil calendar. Most of these are associated with Easter (which is a movable feast), either a certain number of days before (e.g., Lent is 40 days before Easter, excluding Sundays) or after (e.g., Pentecost is 50 days after Easter Sunday). Advent is another moveable feast, which begins the four Sundays prior to December 25th.

Rogation Days: Nearly at the advent of Christianity a custom arose in the Church at Rome for which Christians would process in the city or in the country on specific days of the year in supplication to God for His blessings. They would ask for various intentions, particularly for God's blessing upon them and His protection of their city or town. These days came to be called "Rogation Days," coming from the Latin word *"rogare,"* which means "to ask," or to pray to God for these intentions. Eventually the specific intentions for the Rogation Days became asking God for forgiveness of the sins of the world, for protection against calamities, to bless their fields during the planting season and for a bountiful harvest.

In 1969, nearly four years after the closing of the Second Vatican Council, the Sacred Congregation of Divine Worship published General Norms for the Liturgical Year and the Calendar, which gave the local bishops the authority to adapt these customs to their region. Today, Rogation prayers are said for the needs of all people, for the produce of the earth and for human labor, and for thanksgiving for all of God's blessings.

Rogation Days are celebrated in Divine Worship on the three days following Rogation Sunday, which is the Sixth Sunday of Easter. Rogation Days are celebrated in the Extraordinary Form on the 25th of April and the three days before Ascension Thursday. They are not generally observed in the Ordinary Form, though there is the ability for them to be. They are not observed in the Eastern Rites.

Ember Days: Like Rogation Days, Ember Days are also those on which the Church publicly gives thanks to the Lord for the needs of the people, for productive lands, and for the labor of mankind. However, Ember Days are distinguished by their penitential character. In the Extraordinary Form, observance of Ember Days includes the obligation to abstain from meat and to fast. In Divine Worship, abstaining and fasting are not obligatory, though some sort of penitential practice on these days is encouraged.

Ember Days are celebrated four times per year. They are marked by the four seasons; they are observed on the Wednesday, Friday and Saturday of these four weeks. Ember Days in Divine Worship are observed on the Wednesday, Friday and Saturday during the week of the First Sunday of Lent, the week of Pentecost Sunday, after the 14th of September, and after the 13th of December. They are observed in the Extraordinary Form on the same days as Divine Worship. They are not generally observed in the Ordinary Form, though they can be. They are not observed in the Eastern Rites.

Divine Worship
Personal Ordinariates

The circular diagram shows the liturgical year divided into seasons with their associated colors:
- Advent — Purple
- Christmas — White
- Epiphanytide — Green
- Pre-Lent — Purple
- Lent — Purple
- Easter — White
- Trinitytide — Green

The Liturgical Year at a Glance

- **Advent** begins the liturgical year 4 Sundays before Dec 25th

- **Christmas** is the first great solemnity of the liturgical year always celebrated on December 25th; the solemnity continues for 8 days called the Christmas Octave

- **Epiphany** is celebrated on Jan 6th or the Sunday between Jan 2-8; the Epiphany season continues until the Feast of the Baptism of the Lord, the first Sunday after Jan 6th

- **Time after Epiphany** varies depending upon the date of Easter

- **Pre-Lent** begins the 3rd Sunday before Lent with Septuagesima Sunday

- **Lent** begins with Ash Wednesday (6 weeks before Easter) and ends at the celebration of the Mass of the Lord's Supper on Holy Thursday
  - *Holy Week* begins with Palm Sunday, the Sunday before Easter Sunday
  - *Paschal Triduum* are Holy Thursday, Good Friday, and Holy Saturday

- **Easter** is the great solemnity celebrated on the first Sunday after the first full moon after the Spring Equinox; the solemnity continues for 8 days of the Easter Octave
  - *Pentecost Octave* begins on Pentecost Sunday, 50 days after Easter, until Trinity Sunday

- **Time after Trinity** is the period following Trinity Sunday until the Feast of Christ the King, the last Sunday before Advent

The Liturgical Year at a Glance

- **Advent** begins the liturgical year 4 Sundays before Dec 25th

- **Christmas** is the first great solemnity of the liturgical year always celebrated on December 25th; the solemnity continues for 8 days called the Christmas Octave

- *Christmas season* continues until the Feast of the Baptism of the Lord, the first Sunday after Jan 6th

- **Ordinary Time** varies depending upon the date of Easter; it is interrupted by Lent

- **Lent** begins with Ash Wednesday (6 weeks before Easter) and ends at the celebration of the Mass of the Lord's Supper on Holy Thursday

- *Holy Week* begins with Passion (Palm) Sunday, the Sunday before Easter Sunday

- *Paschal Triduum* are Holy Thursday, Good Friday, and Holy Saturday

- **Easter** is the second great solemnity which is celebrated on the first Sunday after the first full moon after the Spring Equinox; the solemnity continues for 8 days of the Easter Octave

- *Easter Season* continues until Pentecost, 50 days after Easter

- **Ordinary time** resumes and ends with the Feast of Christ the King, the last Sunday before Advent

Ordinary Form

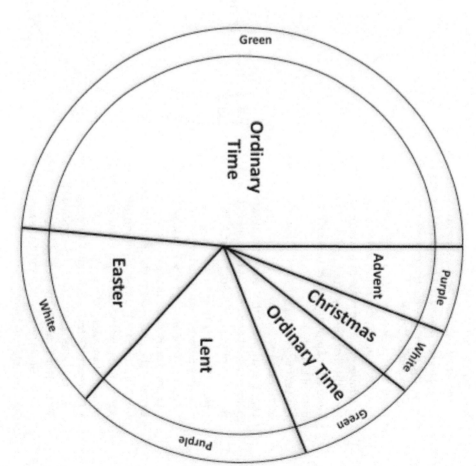

106

The Liturgical Year at a Glance

- **Advent** begins the liturgical year 4 Sundays before Dec 25th

- **Christmastide** is the first great solemnity of the liturgical year always celebrated on December 25th; the solemnity continues for 8 days called the Christmas Octave

  - *Epiphany* is celebrated on Jan 6th or the Sunday between Jan 2–8; the Epiphany season continues until the Feast of the Baptism of the Lord, the first Sunday after Jan 6th

- **Epiphanytide** varies depending upon the date of Easter

- **Pre-Lent** begins the 3rd Sunday before Lent with Septuagesima Sunday

- **Lent** begins with Ash Wednesday (6 weeks before Easter) and ends at the celebration of the Mass of the Lord's Supper on Holy Thursday

  - *Holy Week* begins with Palm Sunday, the Sunday before Easter Sunday

  - *Paschal Triduum* are Holy Thursday, Good Friday, and Holy Saturday

- **Eastertide** is the great solemnity celebrated on the first Sunday after the first full moon after the Spring Equinox; the solemnity continues for 8 days of the Easter Octave

  - *Pentecost Octave* begins on Pentecost Sunday, 50 days after Easter, until Trinity Sunday

- **Season after Pentecost** is the period following Trinity Sunday until Advent

Extraordinary Form

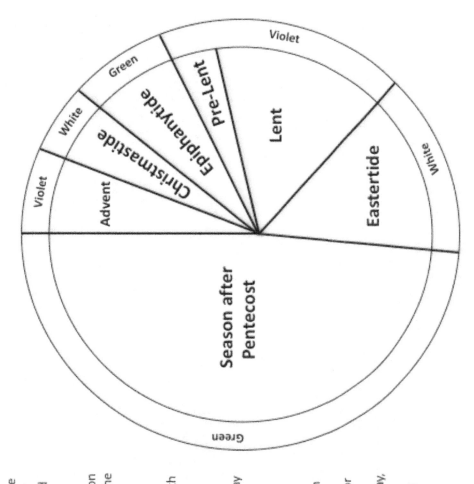

107

The Liturgical Year at a Glance

- **Preparation for the Nativity of Our Lord** begins with the Nativity fast, 40 days before Dec 25th

- **Christmas** is the first great solemnity of the liturgical year always celebrated on December 25th, with the Christmas season continuing until the Theophany (the Epiphany and the Feast of the Baptism of the Lord) on Jan 6th

- **Pre-Paschal Season** varies depending upon the date of Easter; it ends with the **Triodion**, which is the three weeks prior to Lent

- **The Great Fast (The Great Lent)** begins with Clean Monday (7 weeks before Easter) and ends with Holy Week

- **Holy Week** begins with the Monday after Passion (Palm) Sunday, the Sunday before Easter Sunday

- **Paschal Season** begins with Pascha (Easter Sunday), which is calculated differently from the Latin Rite, being the first Sunday after the first full moon, after March 21st; it ends with the Feast of the Holy Trinity

- **Season of Pentecost** Begins after Trinity Sunday, so it does not actually include the Feast of Pentecost (which is 50 days after Pascha); the beginning of the Eastern liturgical year begins either September 1st or 14th

Byzantine Rite
An Eastern Rite of the Catholic Church

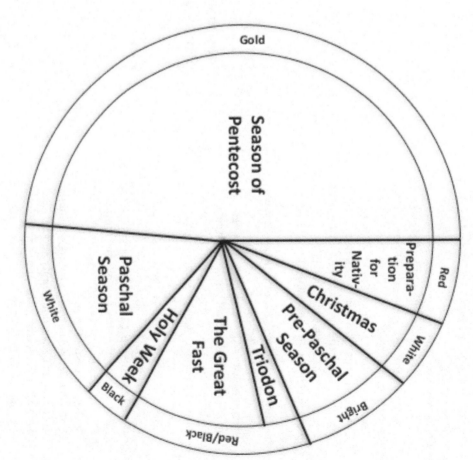

Lent: An Overview

Spring training analogy:

As sports teams use spring training to get "back to the basics" to prepare for the upcoming season, Lent can be viewed in a similar way for training in the spiritual life.

What are we preparing for?

For those not yet baptized, it is a preparation for Baptism which offers eternal life with the Trinity. Baptism is possible only because of Good Friday (the Cross) and Easter Sunday (the Resurrection). Baptism is only for those who have "Repented and believed in the Gospel" (see Mk 1:15). In the case of infants, this belief is professed for them by their parents. Until infants come of age, they are held within the faith of their family.

For those already baptized, it is returning to the basics of repentance and belief. It is ongoing conversion which is not a one-time event but a life long struggle. Christ calls all to holiness: "You must be perfect, as your heavenly Father is perfect" (Mt 5:48). We must always strive for holiness, without which no one will see God (see Heb 12:14). For more see Catechism of the Catholic Church (CCC) 1434-1439; 2012-2016.

What are the basics we get back to?

Prayer, Fasting and Almsgiving are traditional basics for holiness (see CCC 1438-1439; 2043).

Prayer: We cannot know God without a prayer life (see CCC 2744-2745). Prayer life is always in the Church whether praying with others in the community, in a group, or during individual prayer. Prayer is essential if we are to become holy. Lenten traditions of prayer include attending daily Mass as much as possible, additional devotions such as Stations of the Cross and community Rosaries, etc. Read Part 4 of the CCC on prayer (CCC 2558-2758); it is fairly short and is very readable and helpful.

Fasting: "There is no holiness without renunciation and spiritual battle" (CCC 2015). Fasting actually can cover a multitude of practices of renunciation. These are acts of love in which we deny ourselves good things in promises of better (Heaven). When not filled by material goods, we leave room within us for the Holy Spirit. We come to recognize our total dependence upon God for all we have and this makes us humble. Humility is the first step toward holiness. In addition to the minimum requirements, traditional practices are to give up some good to which we might be particularly attached. This should be something that will help us to remember throughout the day that we are totally dependent upon God. Foods are usually the most common sacrifices because of the significance of hunger upon us, but one can sacrifice other things as well. Read CCC 538; 1434; 2043.

Almsgiving: Almsgiving, is an act of love and leads us to want to give all of ourselves to God. This is in addition to the "tithe" we owe to God and His Church on an ongoing basis. A tithe is an offering back to God of the first fruits of what He has given us, in service of His mission. Traditionally the tithe is 10% of our income. Almsgiving can also include acts of mercy whereby we aid our neighbor, especially the poor. The spiritual and corporal works of mercy are traditional practices (see CCC 2447). Read CCC 1434; 2447.

Are these practices just limited to Lent?

The purpose of Lent is to reorient us to the fundamentals of spiritual maturity; however, to strive for holiness (i.e., perfection in our love) we need to make these practices a permanent presence in our everyday lives.

Special Requirements for Lent: Abstinence and Fasting

Abstinence means no meat or meat products (such as broth, etc.). Abstinence is required of all beginning on their 15th birthday. Abstinence is obligatory during every Friday of Lent (throughout the rest of the year, we may substitute some other food or penitential practice instead of abstaining from meat). Fasting means one normal meal and up to two collations (or breaks of the fast) if necessary but the two collations should not add up to one full meal. Fasting is binding on all who are ages 18-59, except those who are ill, pregnant or where it would jeopardize health. Fasting and abstinence are both obligatory on Ash Wednesday and Good Friday.

Holy Week

Holy Week begins with Palm Sunday and culminates with the Triduum (Latin for three days). The Triduum starts on the evening of Holy Thursday when we celebrate the institution of the Eucharist and the institution of the priesthood at the Last Supper. The Mass of the Lord's Supper on Thursday evening will be the last Mass celebrated until the Easter vigil. Traditionally there will be an all-night vigil in front of the Blessed Sacrament which the faithful are invited to attend and pray.

A tradition that arose in Rome in the early Church was the visiting of the seven station churches, known as the Seven Churches Visitation. To celebrate this tradition, pilgrims visit seven area churches before midnight that are keeping the vigil, and say specific prayers commemorating seven of the stations of the Cross.

Good Friday commemorates Christ's Passion and Death on the Cross. There is no Mass, but there is a Liturgy of the Lord's Passion on Good Friday. This is the last day that Stations of the Cross are customarily celebrated during the liturgical year.

There is no Mass on Holy Saturday (the third day of the Triduum) until the Easter Vigil Mass, which is celebrated after sundown. Liturgically, those who celebrate the Easter Vigil have now entered into Easter Sunday.

ORDER OF THE MASS

The most visible differences among Rites, and among variants within Rites, are the Order of the Mass as well as the way the Mass is celebrated. The Missal (a Missal is a book which provides the directions for celebrating the Mass and the prayers to be said) which the Ordinariates use is called Divine Worship. As we discussed earlier, Divine Worship is a variant within the Roman Rite. As such, it has aspects in common with both the Extraordinary Form and the Ordinary Form.

One of the principle sources for Divine Worship is the Book of Common Prayer introduced in 1549 by Archbishop Thomas Cranmer, about 15 years after Henry VIII formally broke unity with Rome and established the schismatic "Church of England." Cranmer is believed to have used the Sarum Missal (the Latin Missal widely in use in England at the time) as the basis of his reformulation of the liturgy. Cranmer's reformulation he called the Book of Common Prayer. In terms of the Mass, the 1549 version was primarily a translation of the Sarum Missal into English. At this point, the Mass of the Book of Common Prayer would not yet have the significant Protestant innovations that would come three years later in the 1552 edition of the Book of Common Prayer.

The Sarum Missal is a variant of the Roman Rite. It was developed by St. Osmund, Bishop of Salisbury in Southern England, in the 11th century (Salisbury was once known as Sarum). St. Osmund wished to keep the Missal true to the Roman Missal, while incorporating a number of Norman liturgical traditions. This Missal came to be used widely throughout England. The Sarum Missal is many centuries older than the Missal of St. Pius V, which was promulgated in the late 16th century. St. Pius V's Missal is the basis of the Extraordinary Form but both Sarum and the Missal of Pius V are grounded in the same Roman traditions. For this reason, Divine Worship and the Extraordinary Form have similarities in many aspects of the Roman Rite that preexisted both Pius V's Missal and the Sarum Missal. They also are commonly celebrated with the same sense of reverence and solemnity.

The Divine Worship Missal is also influenced by the Missal of the Ordinary Form. This influence is in the rubrics (the instructions for the manner in which the Mass is celebrated), and in some of the theological insights the Ordinary Form clarifies that are present in a more unarticulated manner in the Extraordinary Form.

This influence of the Ordinary Form can be seen most readily by looking at the Order of the Mass of both Missals, side-by-side (see the chart on page 113). The structure and the terminology of Divine Worship and the Ordinary Form are the most obviously similar aspects from a first look (e.g., Introductory Rites, Liturgy of the Word, Liturgy of the Eucharist, Concluding Rites). This holds true especially when one looks at all four Masses which we have been studying (i.e., Divine Worship, Ordinary Form,

Extraordinary Form, and Divine Liturgy). One can also see that the order of the Extraordinary Form and the Divine Liturgy have some similarities that are not as apparent when comparing Divine Worship to the Extraordinary Form (e.g., Mass of the Catechumen, Mass of the Faithful). This structure of the Extraordinary Form and Divine Liturgy appear to be much more similar to one another than either of them are to Divine Worship. However, if one participates in these liturgies in person, he will discover that the aesthetic experience of Divine Worship and the Extraordinary Form are much closer to one another than either is to the Divine Liturgy.

Regardless of superficial appearances and aesthetic experiences, all four do have the same fundamental, two-fold division. The first part of the Mass is ordered to the proclamation of the Good News of Jesus Christ, formed around readings from Scripture. The second part of Mass is the action which makes present to the faithful celebrating, the saving action which Christ performed in His public ministry and, most solemnly, in His Passion and death. Within this structure, all four liturgies have most of the same important features; they all have a penitential expression, readings from Scripture, especially the New Testament letters and the Gospel, a homily, the Nicene Creed, preparation of the gifts, a prayer of remembrance, consecration and epiclesis (calling down the Holy Spirit) which transforms bread and wine into the Body and Blood of Christ, the Lord's Prayer, and a rite of receiving Holy Communion.

What we can see from this quick look at the diversity of liturgical expression in the Catholic Church is that there is a profound unity of meaning and structure, even while there are differences in expression. Nevertheless, these differences conform to the meaning of the Mass. Divine Worship fits well within the liturgical patrimony of the Catholic Church, even if some of its distinctive elements were introduced after the break of the Church of England from Rome (e.g., 16th century English language).

Divine Worship also provides an important contribution to the Church and to the Ordinary Form. One of the things that many people notice after attending Divine Worship and then the Ordinary Form is that the common manner of saying Divine Worship returns the solemnity and reverence that seem to be lacking in the way the Ordinary Form is usually offered. Divine Worship shows how beauty in liturgical language, sacred music, and attention to rubrics can help the faithful to realize that in the Mass they are no longer simply on earth, but also in heaven. Being closer to the Ordinary Form in many ways (vernacular language, structure of the Mass, terminology, etc.), Divine Worship is somewhat better suited than the other forms to influence the Ordinary Form toward renewal in order to recover some important liturgical elements that may have been diminished in the wake of the 1970 reform of the liturgy.

Divine Worship	Ordinary Form	Extraordinary Form	Divine Liturgy of St. John Chrysostom

Divine Worship

INTRODUCTORY RITES
- Entrance
- Introit
- Collect for Purity
- Summary of the Law
- Kyrie
- Gloria
- The Collect

LITURGY OF THE WORD
- First Reading (Old Testament)
- Responsorial Psalm
- Second Reading (New Testament)
- Gospel
- The Homily
- The Nicene Creed
- The Prayer of the People
- The Penitential Rite
- The Comfortable Words (optional)
- The Sentences (optional)

LITURGY OF THE EUCHARIST
- The Offertory
- The Prayer over the Offerings
- The Eucharistic Prayer
- The Communion Rite
  - The Lord's Prayer
  - The Rite of Peace
  - The Fraction
  - Agnus Dei
  - Prayer of Humble Access
  - Communion
  - Post Communion Prayers

CONCLUDING RITES
LAST GOSPEL (optional)

Ordinary Form

INTRODUCTORY RITES
- The Entrance
- Greeting of Altar and the People
- Act of Penitence
- Kyrie
- Gloria
- The Collect

LITURGY OF THE WORD
- First Reading (Old Testament)
- Responsorial Psalm
- Second Reading (New Testament)
- Gospel
- The Homily
- The Profession of Faith (Nicene Creed)
- The Prayer of the Faithful

LITURGY OF THE EUCHARIST
- The Preparation of the Gifts
- The Prayer over the Offerings
- The Eucharistic Prayer
- The Communion Rite
  - The Lord's Prayer
  - The Rite of Peace
  - The Fraction
  - Agnus Dei
  - Communion

CONCLUDING RITES

Extraordinary Form

MASS OF THE CATECHUMENS
- Entrance Prayers
- Introit
- Kyrie
- Gloria
- Collect
- Epistle
- Gradual & Alleluia
- Gospel
- Homily
- Credo

MASS OF THE FAITHFUL
- Offertory
- Secret
- Preface
- Sanctus
- Canon
- Communion Rite
- The Lord's Prayer
- Agnus Dei
- Communion
- Post Communion Prayer
- Dismissal
LAST GOSPEL

Divine Liturgy of St. John Chrysostom

PROSKOMEDIA
- Priest prepares gifts at the altar

MASS OF THE CATECHUMENS
- Reverencing Gospel & Altar
- Litany of Peace
- Hymn of the Incarnation
- Third Antiphon
- Little Entrance
- Tropars and Kondaks
- Prayer of Thrice Holy God
- Thrice Holy Hymn
- Epistle
- Gospel
- Homily
- Litany of Supplication

MASS OF THE FAITHFUL
- First Prayer of the Faithful
- Second Prayer of the Faithful
- Cherubimic Hymn
- The Great Entrance
- Litany of the Offertory
- Nicene Creed
- Consecration
- The Epiclesis
- Hymn to the Blessed Virgin
- Litany of Intercession
- Priest's Prayer for Worthy Communion
- The Lord's Prayer
- Communion
- Prayer of Thanksgiving
- Dismissal

How to recite the Holy Rosary

1. SAY THESE PRAYERS...

IN THE NAME of the Father, and of the Son, and of the Holy Spirit. Amen. *(As you say this, with your right hand touch your forehead when you say* Father, *touch your breastbone when you say* Son, *touch your left shoulder when you say* Holy, *and touch your right shoulder when you say* Spirit.*)*

I BELIEVE IN GOD, the Father almighty, Creator of Heaven and earth. And in Jesus Christ, His only Son, our Lord, Who was conceived by the Holy Spirit, born of the Virgin Mary, suffered under Pontius Pilate; was crucified, died, and was buried. He descended into Hell. The third day He rose again from the dead. He ascended into Heaven, and sits at the right hand of God, the Father almighty. He shall come again to judge the living and the dead. I believe in the Holy Spirit, the holy Catholic Church, the communion of saints, the forgiveness of sins, the resurrection of the body, and life everlasting. Amen.

OUR FATHER, Who art in Heaven, hallowed be Thy Name. Thy kingdom come, Thy will be done on earth as it is in Heaven. Give us this day our daily bread, and forgive us our trespasses, as we forgive those who trespass against us. And lead us not into temptation, but deliver us from evil. Amen.

HAIL MARY, full of grace, the Lord is with thee. Blessed art thou among women, and blessed is the fruit of thy womb, Jesus. Holy Mary, Mother of God, pray for us sinners, now and at the hour of our death. Amen.

GLORY BE to the Father, and to the Son, and to the Holy Spirit. As it was in the beginning is now, and ever shall be, world without end. Amen.

O MY JESUS, forgive us our sins, save us from the fires of Hell; lead all souls to Heaven, especially those in most need of Thy mercy. Amen.

HAIL HOLY QUEEN, mother of mercy; our life, our sweetness, and our hope. To thee do we cry, poor banished children of Eve. To thee do we send up our sighs, mourning and weeping in this vale of tears. Turn, then, most gracious advocate, thine eyes of mercy toward us. And after this, our exile, show unto us the blessed fruit of thy womb, Jesus. O clement, O loving, O sweet Virgin Mary. Pray for us, O holy Mother of God, that we may be made worthy of the promises of Christ. Amen.

O GOD, WHOSE only-begotten Son by His life, death and resurrection, has purchased for us the rewards of eternal life; grant, we beseech Thee, that by meditating upon these mysteries of the Most Holy Rosary of the Blessed Virgin Mary, we may imitate what they contain and obtain what they promise, through the same Christ our Lord. Amen.

ANNOUNCE *each mystery by saying something like, "The third Joyful Mystery is the Birth of Our Lord." This is required only when saying the Rosary in a group.*

2. IN THIS ORDER...

INTRODUCTION
1. IN THE NAME...
2. I BELIEVE IN GOD...
3. OUR FATHER...
4. HAIL MARY...
5. HAIL MARY...
6. HAIL MARY...
7. GLORY BE...
8. O MY JESUS...

THE FIRST DECADE
9. ANNOUNCE...
10. OUR FATHER...
11. HAIL MARY...
12. HAIL MARY...
13. HAIL MARY...
14. HAIL MARY...
15. HAIL MARY...
16. HAIL MARY...
17. HAIL MARY...
18. HAIL MARY...
19. HAIL MARY...
20. HAIL MARY...
21. GLORY BE...
22. O MY JESUS...

THE SECOND DECADE
23. ANNOUNCE...
24. OUR FATHER...
25. HAIL MARY...
26. HAIL MARY...
27. HAIL MARY...
28. HAIL MARY...
29. HAIL MARY...
30. HAIL MARY...
31. HAIL MARY...
32. HAIL MARY...
33. HAIL MARY...
34. HAIL MARY...
35. GLORY BE...
36. O MY JESUS...

THE THIRD DECADE
37. ANNOUNCE...
38. OUR FATHER...
39. HAIL MARY...
40. HAIL MARY...
41. HAIL MARY...
42. HAIL MARY...
43. HAIL MARY...
44. HAIL MARY...
45. HAIL MARY...
46. HAIL MARY...
47. HAIL MARY...
48. HAIL MARY...
49. GLORY BE...
50. O MY JESUS...

THE FOURTH DECADE
51. ANNOUNCE...
52. OUR FATHER...
53. HAIL MARY...
54. HAIL MARY...
55. HAIL MARY...
56. HAIL MARY...
57. HAIL MARY...
58. HAIL MARY...
59. HAIL MARY...
60. HAIL MARY...
61. HAIL MARY...
62. HAIL MARY...
63. GLORY BE...
64. O MY JESUS...

THE FIFTH DECADE
65. ANNOUNCE...
66. OUR FATHER...
67. HAIL MARY...
68. HAIL MARY...
69. HAIL MARY...
70. HAIL MARY...
71. HAIL MARY...
72. HAIL MARY...
73. HAIL MARY...
74. HAIL MARY...
75. HAIL MARY...
76. HAIL MARY...
77. GLORY BE...
78. O MY JESUS...

CONCLUSION
79. HAIL HOLY QUEEN...
80. O GOD, WHOSE...
81. IN THE NAME...

3. WHILE TOUCHING THESE BEADS TO KEEP TRACK OF YOUR PROGRESS...

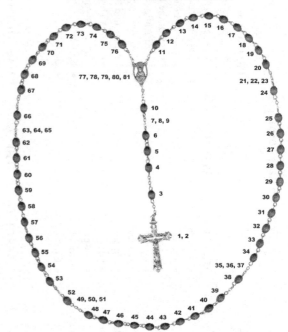

4. AND SILENTLY MEDITATING ON THESE "MYSTERIES", OR EVENTS FROM THE LIVES OF JESUS AND MARY...

On Monday and Saturday, meditate on the "Joyful Mysteries"
First Decade (Steps 9-22): The Annunciation of Gabriel to Mary (Luke 1:26-38)
Second Decade (Steps 23-36): The Visitation of Mary to Elizabeth (Luke 1:39-56)
Third Decade (Steps 37-50): The Birth of Our Lord (Luke 2:1-21)
Fourth Decade (Steps 51-64): The Presentation of Our Lord (Luke 2:22-38)
Fifth Decade (Steps 65-78): The Finding of Our Lord in the Temple (Luke 2:41-52)

On Thursday, meditate on the "Luminous Mysteries"
First Decade: The Baptism of Our Lord in the River Jordan (Matthew 3:13-16)
Second Decade: The Wedding at Cana, when Christ manifested Himself (Jn 2:1-11)
Third Decade: The Proclamation of the Kingdom of God (Mark 1:14-15)
Fourth Decade: The Transfiguration of Our Lord (Matthew 17:1-8)
Fifth Decade: The Last Supper, when Our Lord gave us the Holy Eucharist (Mt 26)

On Tuesday and Friday, meditate on the "Sorrowful Mysteries"
First Decade: The Agony of Our Lord in the Garden (Matthew 26:36-56)
Second Decade: Our Lord is Scourged at the Pillar (Matthew 27:26)
Third Decade: Our Lord is Crowned with Thorns (Matthew 27:27-31)
Fourth Decade: Our Lord Carries the Cross to Calvary (Matthew 27:32)
Fifth Decade: The Crucifixion of Our Lord (Matthew 27:33-56)

On Wednesday and Sunday, meditate on the "Glorious Mysteries"
First Decade: The Glorious Resurrection of Our Lord (John 20:1-29)
Second Decade: The Ascension of Our Lord (Luke 24:36-53)
Third Decade: The Descent of the Holy Spirit at Pentecost (Acts 2:1-41)
Fourth Decade: The Assumption of Mary into Heaven
Fifth Decade: The Coronation of Mary as Queen of Heaven and Earth

You are encouraged to copy and distribute this sheet.

www.newadvent.org

The Chaplet of the Divine Mercy

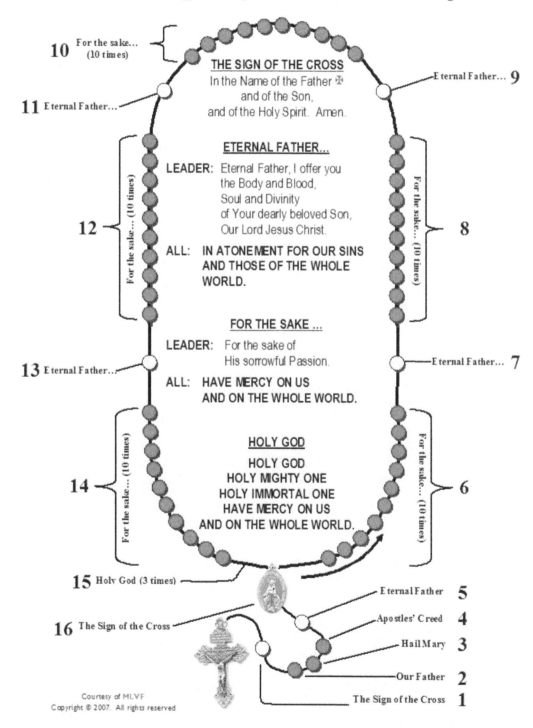

10 For the sake... (10 times)

11 Eternal Father...

12 For the sake... (10 times)

13 Eternal Father...

14 For the sake... (10 times)

15 Holy God (3 times)

16 The Sign of the Cross

THE SIGN OF THE CROSS
In the Name of the Father ✠
and of the Son,
and of the Holy Spirit. Amen.

ETERNAL FATHER...

LEADER: Eternal Father, I offer you
the Body and Blood,
Soul and Divinity
of Your dearly beloved Son,
Our Lord Jesus Christ.

ALL: IN ATONEMENT FOR OUR SINS
AND THOSE OF THE WHOLE
WORLD.

FOR THE SAKE ...

LEADER: For the sake of
His sorrowful Passion.

ALL: HAVE MERCY ON US
AND ON THE WHOLE WORLD.

HOLY GOD
HOLY GOD
HOLY MIGHTY ONE
HOLY IMMORTAL ONE
HAVE MERCY ON US
AND ON THE WHOLE WORLD.

Eternal Father... **9**

For the sake... (10 times) **8**

Eternal Father... **7**

For the sake... (10 times) **6**

Eternal Father **5**

Apostles' Creed **4**

Hail Mary **3**

Our Father **2**

The Sign of the Cross **1**

115

NOTES

SESSION 10: THE SACRAMENTS OF INITIATION I – BAPTISM & CONFIRMATION

READING ASSIGNMENT

Pages 75-81: questions 250-270

STUDY QUESTIONS

Baptism:

- How does Baptism change who I am? (CCCC q: 263)
- Why is Baptism said to be the first intimate encounter with Jesus Christ? (CCCC q: 252)
- How do the effects of Baptism relate to my desire for happiness? (CCCC qq: 261-263)
- What does dying to my previous life and rising with Christ mean for the rest of my life? (CCCC qq: 252, 263)
- How must I respond to the grace received in Baptism? (CCCC qq: 252-253)

Confirmation:

- How does Confirmation complete my incorporation into Christ? (CCCC qq: 265-266)
- How do the fruits of Confirmation aid in the plan God has for me? (CCCC q: 268)

NOTES:

TUTORIAL ON BAPTISM AND CONFIRMATION

Sacraments of Initiation Overview

The three-fold Sacraments of Initiation are ordered to Trinitarian life and to this life of the Trinity brought to the world in Salvation History. These three Sacraments bring individual human persons into the Trinity's eternal life through the Incarnation and Pentecost. In Baptism we are incorporated into the Son's eternal return of Himself to the Father, which is mediated to us through the Incarnation and especially the Cross. When we are baptized, we die with Jesus Christ to the fallen created order, we promise to continue to die to our fallen selves (i.e., sin) throughout our lives, and so we rise to new life with Christ. When we share in His resurrection, we enter with Him into His "new creation," communion with the Trinity which His obedient Passion and death brought back into the created order.

The second Sacrament of Initiation is Confirmation. In receiving this Sacrament, we are sealed in the Holy Spirit by being incorporated into His ongoing communion of Trinitarian love. Reception of Confirmation completes our baptismal grace and prepares us for full life as a disciple of Christ. The final Sacrament of Initiation is the Eucharist. The Eucharist completes initiation and provides ongoing incorporation and nourishing in Trinitarian life. All of the Sacraments are ordered to the Eucharist and they receive their efficacy from it. In this session, we will look at Baptism and Confirmation.

Baptism

Baptism is each human person's gateway to the eternal life of the Trinity in Jesus Christ. It is the basis for the whole of Christian life and the gateway to life in the Spirit. Baptism frees us from sin (original and personal) and through Baptism we are reborn as sons of God. Baptism makes us members of Christ, it incorporates us into the Church, and commits us as sharers in her mission.

Baptism is called the Sacrament of regeneration and enlightenment. It is regeneration because in it we die with Christ to sin and rise to new life in the Trinity through Him. It is enlightenment because we are enlightened and become sons of light and by means of Light Himself which the Church provides us through catechetical instruction. However, this catechesis already requires the recipient has received the light of faith.

Baptism is necessary for salvation and this is why Jesus commands it of His disciples for all those not yet baptized (see Mt 28:19-20; Mk 16:15-16). Through this Sacrament, the recipient receives a character, a permanent "mark" of incorporation into Christ. For this reason, Baptism can be received only once.

The baptized Christian receives the fruit of justification by which all sins are forgiven. This includes original sin and all personal sins committed up to the time of one's Baptism. In addition, the recipient is also sanctified and all punishment due to sin is remitted, which would allow the recipient direct entry to heaven if there were to be no further personal sin before his death.

Justification and Sanctification are two inseparable aspects of the same process of salvation. Initial justification is given at baptism and incorporates the newly baptized into the life of the Spirit. What we can call ongoing justification is maintaining and deepening our justification through works of love and participation in grace (or returning to the state of grace through the Sacrament of Reconciliation, which is the state of communion with Christ). Sanctification is the other side of the coin of justification. It can never be separate from justification. Rather, sanctification is that aspect of the process of salvation by which our works of love and self-mastery cause us to increasingly conform ourselves to Christ. This entire process is of God's initiative and comes about through our active cooperation with Him.

To be validly baptized, the recipient must be immersed or infused in water, in which a minister says the Trinitarian formula of Baptism. The most expressive form is triple immersion because it symbolizes the recipient's death to sin and his resurrection to new life. Infusion is more common form. Here the minister pours water over the head of the recipient three times as he says the Trinitarian formula: "I baptize you in the name of the Father, and of the Son and of the Holy Spirit." This is the form. The matter is water consecrated at Easter Vigil or at the time of Baptism, through the prayer of epiclesis (i.e., the calling down of the Holy Spirit upon the waters of Baptism).

Those who are ready to receive Baptism must commit themselves in faith to Christ. Baptized infants are incorporated into Christ within their parents' faith, until they can maturely embrace this faith for themselves. Therefore, both adults and children require formation in faith beginning with initial proclamation (the kerygma) to achieve an initial faith, and then through catechesis to mature and deepen their incipient faith.

Baptism shows that faith is never a private matter. As the faith itself must be mediated by other members of the Church, so must Baptism: no one is able to baptize himself. The ordinary ministers of Baptism are bishops, priests, and deacons. In serious circumstances, extraordinary ministers can be an appointed by the bishop. For example, a layperson can be appointed to perform Baptisms in remote locations without a priest or deacon. In the case of grave necessity, anyone can baptize. Even a non-baptized person can baptize as long as he uses the right form and matter, and has the intention to do what the Church does.

Confirmation

Confirmation is necessary for the completion of baptismal grace. Through Confirmation, the Christian is bound more perfectly to the Church, especially strengthened by the Holy Spirit, and more firmly obligated to spread and defend the faith by word and deed. The relationship between Confirmation and the sending of the

Holy Spirit at Pentecost is a parallel to the connection between Baptism and Christ's Incarnation, Passion and Death on the Cross.

Confirmation was originally integrated with Baptism in the early Church forming a kind of double-Sacrament. In the West, the desire to keep Confirmation's connection with the Bishop as the presence of Christ in the local Church causes the two become temporally separated. In the East, the concern to show their unity has kept them integrated and so the priest is permitted to Confirm (which they call chrismation) as an ordinary minister using with the oil (myron) blessed by the bishop. There was double anointing in the Western tradition after Baptism, which facilitated the temporal separation of Baptism and Confirmation. However, the West always understood the second anointing to be that which was efficacious (i.e., which effects Confirmation).

Like Baptism, Confirmation also imprints an indelible mark on the soul and so is also given only once. It perfects the recipient in the common priesthood of the faithful, which they received in Baptism. The fruits of Confirmation include rooting the Christian more deeply in divine sonship, uniting him more firmly to Christ, rendering his bond to the Church more perfect, increasing in him the gifts of the Holy Spirit, and giving him a special strength to spread and defend the faith by word and action.

The essential aspects of Confirmation include the form, which are the words spoken by the minister: "Be sealed with the gift of the Holy Spirit," and the proper matter, which is anointing with sacred chrism on the forehead and the laying on of the hands. The rite ends with the sign of peace between the bishop and faithful manifesting their ecclesial communion.

Every baptized person not yet confirmed can and should be confirmed. A Christian's initiation is not complete without this Sacrament. All Christians in danger of death should be confirmed, even to children who have not yet reached the age of reason.

Confirmandi must be in a state of grace to receive Confirmation, so they should receive the Sacrament of Penance before Confirmation. The Candidate should have the spiritual assistance of a sponsor to help him prepare for the Sacrament. It is appropriate for the godparents also to be a Confirmation sponsor in order to show the connection between the two Sacraments.

The ordinary minister of Confirmation is the bishop in the West (the original minister) and the bishop or priest in the East. Only Orthodox Chrismation and Catholic Confirmation/Chrismation are valid. In danger of death or with permission, in the West the priest is an extraordinary minister of Confirmation.

NOTES

SESSION 11: THE SACRAMENTS OF INITIATION II – THE MOST HOLY EUCHARIST

READING ASSIGNMENT

Pages 81-86: questions 271-294

STUDY QUESTIONS

The Most Holy Eucharist:

- What does the Eucharist say about God's love for me and my human family? (CCCC q: 271)
- How can I understand the Eucharist as a Sacrifice and as a Sacrament? (CCCC qq: 280-281)
- What does the Real Presence of Jesus Christ in the Eucharist mean for the intimacy into which God calls me? (CCCC q: 283)
- What does the relationship between Sacrifice and Love mean for the way I must live my life? (CCCC qq: 280-281)
- What does the Eucharist say about the relationship between love and life? (CCCC qq: 280, 281, 294)

NOTES:

TUTORIAL ON THE EUCHARIST

The Eucharist

The term Eucharist derives from the Greek word *eucharistia*, which means "thanksgiving." Thanksgiving is an action rooted in the Son's eternal act of thanksgiving to the Father in the life of the Trinity. The Son as Thanksgiving breaks into the world in the Incarnation and is especially manifested in Jesus Christ's passion, death, resurrection and ascension into heaven. The Sacrament of the Eucharist, celebrated in the Holy Sacrifice of the Mass, makes these events of thanksgiving in salvation history (especially the passion, death and resurrection) present on the altar.

For these reasons the Catechism of the Catholic Church (CCC) calls the Eucharist the source and summit of Christian life. It is the source of Christian life because it is Christ Jesus who is present Body, Blood, Soul and Divinity under the signs of bread and wine. The Eucharist is also the summit because Christ is present, Who is the very foundation of our lives as Christians. It is also the summit because in receiving the Eucharist we enter into an ineffable communion with Our Bridegroom and so we are united into the Communion of the Church and at the same time, we are incorporated into the very life of the Trinity.

The Eucharist completes Christian initiation by renewing and deepening the individual Christian into the ongoing participation of the members of the Body of Christ in the Paschal Mystery and Trinitarian Life. For these reasons, the CCC says that the Eucharist makes the Church. It "makes the Church" because it is both the sign and cause of communion of the People of God in divine life and of the unity among the members which keeps the Church in being in the created order.

St. John Paul II said that the Eucharist is above all a sacrifice. There is a close relationship between the Old Testament types of the Eucharist and their fulfillment in the New Testament. Melchizedek's offering of bread and wine as a sacrifice (see Gen 14:18) is fulfilled in Jesus Christ. Jesus begins His Sacrifice in the upper room in His offering of bread and wine, which He says is His Body and Blood. It is His Sacrifice of praise and thanksgiving that restores both mankind and the world to God because it is nothing less than the one Sacrifice of Calvary, made present on the altar, and applied to the Church in time. The Sacrifice of the Mass makes present, that is it *re-presents,* the one Sacrifice of the Cross which is offered for not only those present, but for all the Church Militant and Suffering.

Communion is the very being of the Trinitarian God Who is a Communion of three Persons. Communion is the very being of Jesus Christ Who unites within Himself divinity with humanity. Jesus offers us communion with God through the Church and in the ongoing event we call the Sacrament of the Eucharist. Our communion with Jesus Christ and the Trinity reaches its greatest height of intimacy in the Mass and particularly in

Holy Communion in which we join ourselves—body and soul, to Him—Body, Blood, Soul, and Divinity. Because we are incorporated into the life of the Trinity in the Eucharist, we also participate and anticipate the heavenly kingdom that we will experience at the end of time.

Celebration of the Eucharist

The Mass for all ages. While many non-essential elements have changed through the years, the essential structure of the Mass has continued from the early Church. The CCC quotes St. Justin Martyr, writing in the middle of the second century, in which he outlines the order of the Eucharistic celebration. St. Justin was writing to the pagan emperor Antoninus Pius (AD 138-161) around the year AD 155, explaining what Christians did:

> *On the day we call the day of the sun, all who dwell in the city or country gather in the same place. The memoirs of the apostles and the writings of the prophets are read, as much as time permits. When the reader has finished, he who presides over those gathered admonishes and challenges them to imitate these beautiful things. Then we all rise together and offer prayers* for ourselves . . .and for all others, wherever they may be, so that we may be found righteous by our life and actions, and faithful to the commandments, so as to obtain eternal salvation. When the prayers are concluded we exchange the kiss. Then someone brings bread and a cup of water and wine mixed together to him who presides over the brethren. He takes them and offers praise and glory to the Father of the universe, through the name of the Son and of the Holy Spirit and for a considerable time he gives thanks (in Greek: eucharistian) that we have been judged worthy of these gifts. When he has concluded the prayers and thanksgivings, all present give voice to an acclamation by saying: 'Amen.' When he who presides has given thanks and the people have responded, those whom we call deacons give to those present the "eucharisted" bread, wine and water and take them to those who are absent (CCC 1345).*

St. Justin's explanation to the emperor reveals the essential elements of the Mass the Church has guarded for over 2000 years. The overall organization is comprised of two major movements, which today we call the Liturgy of the Word and the Liturgy of the Eucharist. These two movements perhaps we might not call parts but aspects of the Mass, because they are inseparable aspects of one, seamless essential unity. The two aspects are: (1) the assembly of the faithful leading to the Liturgy of the Word comprised of: readings, homily and general intercessions; (2) the Liturgy of the Eucharist comprised of: the presentation of the bread and wine, the consecratory thanksgiving, and Holy Communion. Together these two movements comprise "one single act of worship."

The CCC describes the relationship of Jesus Christ to His Body, the Church in celebrating the Mass. It says that Jesus acts through His priest, who acts *in persona Christi Capitis*: *"...At its head is Christ himself, the principal agent of the Eucharist. He is high priest of the New Covenant; it is he himself who presides invisibly over every Eucharistic celebration. It is in representing him that the bishop or priest acting in the person of Christ the head (in persona Christi capitis) presides over the assembly, speaks after the readings, receives the offerings, and says the Eucharistic Prayer. All have their own active parts to play in the celebration, each in his own way: readers, those who bring up the offerings, those who give communion, and the whole people whose "Amen" manifests their participation"* (CCC 1348).

The essential aspects of the Mass are its form, or the necessary words the priest (or bishop) must speak for Transubstantiation (see below) to occur. The valid minister must say the words of epiclesis and words of consecration for the Mass to valid. Valid matter must be used, which must include both wheat bread (it can be made only of water and wheat, nothing else can be added or changed without compromising its validity) and grape wine (no additives or other sources of wine may be used). Valid ministers are only validly ordained bishops or priests (we will discuss this more when we cover Holy Orders in Session 13).

A Scriptural Description of the Mass as Sacrifice (the basic structure follows Scott Hahn's *Fourth Cup*)

The celebration of the Mass of the Lord's Supper on Holy Thursday reveals to us that the Mass arises out of the Old Testament Passover seder that Jesus transforms into the New Testament Eucharist (see Jn 19:30; Lk 22:15; Mk 14:22-15:23). The Passover seder was a sacrificial meal, in which the family celebrated the covenant of communion with God by means of the Passover Lamb that had been slain and offered on the altar in the Temple in Jerusalem. The Passover Lamb was about the People of God being rescued from slavery, not simply physical but spiritual slavery to the gods of Egypt. Their sacrifice was about trust in God by rejecting the gods of Egypt, and in response God brings them out of slavery to communion with Him in the Covenant.

Sacrifice is an act of total self-gift. Because of the fallen world, it is not unusual for us to experience total, self-giving love together with some sort of loss. However, while we might lose something associated with the fallen world, authentic love is never real loss. Rather, total self-giving love is the only way that we find ourselves and fulfill our potential as persons, which is to love perfectly. The Cross is the consummation of the total gift Jesus makes of Himself throughout His entire life, beginning with the Incarnation and throughout His public ministry. John's Gospel makes this connection: "Greater love has no man than this, to lay down His life for His friends" (Jn 15:13); "I lay down my life for the Sheep" (Jn 10:15) and this is why the Father loves Him (Jn 10:17).

Scripture clearly shows that the Last Supper was a Passover seder celebration: Luke 22:15: *"And he said to them, 'I have earnestly desired to eat this Passover with you before I suffer.'"* Mark's Gospel shows us something about the Passover Seder that is not explicit in the Old Testament, but it conforms with the Rabbinic tradition (see Tractate *Pesahim*). Mark says that after Jesus had offered bread, which He called His Body and a chalice of wine, which he says is His Blood of the Covenant, He says He will not drink again of the fruit of the vine until He drinks it new in the Kingdom. Then they sing a hymn and go out to the Mount of Olives (see Mk 14:22-26). The Rabbis in Tractate *Pesahim* show that in the Passover seder there are four cups of wine drunk that comprise the basic liturgical structure of the Passover meal.

The first cup is taken for the *kadush* (a blessing). Psalm 113 (which they call the little Hallel Psalm) is then sung. The second cup is then drunk for the *magid*, which is the telling of the story of God's deliverance of Israel from Egypt. The third cup is called the "cup of blessing." Those present consume the third cup after prayers of thanksgiving are given over the cup and unleavened bread. Then the Great Hallel Psalms (Psalm 114-117) are sung. After this "hymn" is sung, everyone present must now drink the fourth cup, called the "cup of consummation." Everyone must drink this cup because it brings the seder to its *consummation*. If we refer back to Mark's Gospel, we see something very remarkable. The fourth cup is not taken. In fact, we saw Jesus say that they would not be drinking it. He would only drink the cup of consummation when He drinks it new in the Kingdom.

With the cup of blessing, as we will see, His Passion has now begun. In His Passion, we are shown a number of times Jesus makes reference to a cup. In the garden of Gethsemane, He asks the Father if it be possible to "remove this cup" (Mk 14:32). This is the third cup of suffering, His Blood of the Covenant, which He must drink to the dregs. From the garden, Jesus is arrested, tried, convicted, scourged and sentenced to die an unbelievably horrible death by crucifixion. On His way of the Cross, He is offered wine mixed with *myrrh,* but he does not drink it (see Mk 15:23); the Kingdom of Heaven has not yet arrived. It is at the end of His Passion that we see it is time for the fourth cup, the cup of consummation.

John records that when Jesus saw all was now consummated, in order to fulfill Scripture, He says "I thirst" (Jn 19: 28). He is given new wine, the third cup of His suffering (and our blessing) has mercifully now come to an end. He drinks the new wine from a sponge and gives up His spirit. All is now consummated (finished) and He is able to drink the cup of consummation new in the Kingdom of God. The Passion begins in the upper room when He holds Himself in His own hands as St. Thomas Aquinas writes in the part of his Eucharistic poem which is commonly referred to as the *Pange lingua*. His Sacrifice on the Cross and the "Passover Seder become the Mass" are one and the same event. It is this New Testament Passover that brings the eternal grace of that 2000-year-old bloody Sacrifice, present in an unbloody but real manner.

The Mass as a Perpetual Sacrificial Offering in Scripture

Scripture also shows us that the "Passover become the Sacrifice of the Mass" is to be continued to be celebrated. In fact, we hear it from Jesus very lips. He tells His disciples at the Last Supper to "do this in memory of Me." This command hearkens back to God's command to Moses and Israel throughout Numbers 9:2-14 and 8 and 2 Chronicles 30:1-5; 35:1, 16-18 to keep the Passover sacrificial memorial. Moreover, the rabbis say that the Passover memorial is to be understood not as a distant memory of something that has long since past, but as a sort of mystical participation in the one Passover celebrated with Moses and Israel in Egypt. This is implied by Moses' command to Israel in the Book of Exodus: *"And you shall tell your son on that day, 'It is because of what the Lord did for me when I came out of Egypt.' ...You shall therefore keep this ordinance at its appointed time from year to year"* (Exodus 13:8, 10). Note that every Jew in subsequent ages who prays these words of the of Exodus Passover at his own Passover seder (i.e., the *magid*), when he says *"what the Lord did for me,"* speaks as if he were there at the historical Passover. This is what Jesus presupposes in His command to His newly ordained bishops to keep offering/celebrating this New Testament Passover—the Sacrifice of the Mass—in His memory. Every bishop and priest who prays the Jesus' words of the New Testament Passover at Mass, is there with Jesus at the first Mass in the Upper Room . . . and Jesus is there in the person of the bishop and priest who is speaking in the Person of Christ.

We can see that the New Testament Church took Jesus' command in exactly this way. The author to the Epistle to the Hebrews writes: *"Let us hold fast the confession of our hope without wavering, for he who promised is faithful; and let us consider how to stir up one another to love and good works, not neglecting to meet together, as is the habit of some, but encouraging one another, and all the more as you see the Day drawing near. For if we sin deliberately after receiving the knowledge of the truth, there no longer remains a sacrifice for sins . . ."* (Heb 10:23-26).

This passage warns us that we sin deliberately by neglecting to meet together because in doing so we are rejecting the knowledge of some truth. But what truth? Well it would seem to have to do with the Jesus' sacrifice for our sins. The passage continues: *" . . . but a fearful prospect of judgment, and a fury of fire which will consume the adversaries. A man who has violated the law of Moses dies without mercy at the testimony of two or three witnesses. How much worse punishment do you think will be deserved by the man who has spurned the Son of God, and profaned the blood of the covenant by which he was sanctified, and outraged the Spirit of grace?"* (Heb 27-29).

The phrase "Blood of the Covenant" is used by Jesus only one time. We saw Him use it to institute the Eucharist in the upper room.

The author of the epistle explains that "the knowledge of the truth" is also the meaning of the Blood of the Covenant. If we neglect to meet together after receiving the knowledge of the truth - that Jesus' sacrifice was the only sacrifice that saves us from our sins - then we reject it by rejecting his command to "do this in remembrance of Me." If we don't go to Mass, we are saying we don't need His Sacrifice. But the author of Hebrews warns us if we reject Jesus' sacrifice by not meeting together, there is no other sacrifice we can turn to. If we neglect to meet together as has become the habit of some, we profane the blood of the covenant and outrage the Spirit of grace. The author of the epistle to the Hebrews explains the Mass is not an optional assembly. Rather, it is necessary for salvation because it makes present to Christians, the Sacrifice of the Cross by which we have access to the Blood of the Covenant through which we may be saved. It is the Mass that applies to members of the Body of Christ, throughout time, the grace of the Cross.

The Real Presence and Its Foundation in Scripture

The Church teaches that Jesus Christ is present in the Eucharist in a way that surpasses every other way He is present on earth with us today. In the Eucharist He is present: Body, Blood, Soul and Divinity. This unique mode of Jesus' presence in the Eucharist places it above all of the other Sacraments. This is because in it, the Catechism says, *"the body and blood, together with the soul and divinity, of our Lord Jesus Christ and, therefore, the whole Christ is truly, really and substantially contained"* (CCC 1374).

The Christian theological tradition coined a term to describe the reality of Jesus Christ's real presence in the Eucharist, focusing on the manner in which bread and wine become His Body, Blood, Soul and Divinity. This term is called transubstantiation. The CCC describes it this way: *"The Council of Trent summarizes the Catholic faith by declaring: '... that by the consecration of the bread and wine there takes place a change of the whole substance of the bread into the substance of the body of Christ our Lord and of the whole substance of the wine into the substance of his blood. This change the holy Catholic Church has fittingly and properly called transubstantiation'"* (CCC 1376).

The first place we must go to in order to see this in Scripture is Jesus' words to the crowds of people who came to Him after He had multiplied the fishes and loaves in a lonely place on the northeastern side of the Sea of Galilee in what we call the Bread of Life Discourse (see Jn 6:50-66). The location of this passage is the synagogue in the town of Capernaum and the time is the Passover, probably one year before His Passion. The previous night Jesus had walked on the water of the Sea of Galilee crossing over to the town of Capernaum after having fed the crowd that day with the miracle of the multiplication of loaves and fishes (see Jn 6:1-15). This is the following day; the crowd has followed Him across the Sea of Galilee and found Him in the synagogue.

The crowd asks for sign that He is indeed the Messiah, something they had been sure of the previous day. They pointed to Moses who gave Israel manna from heaven when the people were complaining of a lack of food. Jesus responds that it was His Father not Moses Who gave them the manna. However, Israel ate of it and died, but Jesus says that the true bread from heaven is His flesh which He gives for the life of the world. Those who eat His flesh will not die but have everlasting life. The Jews are taken aback, asking among themselves how Jesus can give His flesh to eat. Jesus' response is shocking. First, it is important to note that a few chapters earlier, Nicodemas had come to Him at night for fear of the Jews. Jesus told Nicodemas that only those who are born anew can see the Kingdom of Heaven in response to Nicodemas' confusion about how one would reenter his mother's womb. Jesus explained that being born again meant baptism, by which one is reborn as a son of the Kingdom through the power of the water and the Holy Spirit. In the following passages of the Bread of the Life discourse, Jesus makes it clear to the crowd of Jews that He does not speak figuratively.

In response to the Jew's murmuring Jesus says "Amen, Amen" to emphasize that they have correctly understood Him. He then says that only those who eat His flesh and drink His blood will have eternal life (see Jn 6:53). To emphasize this, John in the original Greek now changes the term he uses for "to eat" (beginning at John 6:54). The next four times that John reports Jesus saying that His disciples have to eat His flesh, the Greek word is now *trogo*. The conventional word in Greek for human eating, which John had been using, was *phago*. He changes to *trogo*, which is emphasizes eating as gnawing or chewing. Indeed, it is a term used primarily to describe animal eating during the New Testament period to illustrate the reality of eating that Jesus is teaching (although it is now a common term for human eating). John is emphasizing the real, physical eating that will have to be done.

Jesus declares that His flesh is true food and His blood is true drink, and that it must be eaten and drunk if we are to be raised up on the last day. Those who ate the manna in the wilderness died, those who eat this true food will have everlasting life. Another important event now occurs (see Jn 6:60-63). It is no longer the Jews who He had fed the previous day who are murmuring at this incredible teaching. It is now His disciples who join in, saying: *"This is a hard saying; who can listen to it?"* (Jn 6:60). His disciples who have been with him perhaps the entire two years of His public ministry, are now beginning to falter in their faith. Recall that Jesus has explained to these disciples all of the parables that He does not explain to the people. He has sent them out to preach and given them power over demons and beasts of the earth. Jesus even cleared up the misunderstanding of the fearful disciple Nicodemas who would only come out at night. Here, Jesus' response is unmistakable, and they understand Him quite clearly.

He asks His disciples if they have taken offense at this. He then asks: *"Then what if you were to see the Son of man ascending where he was before? It is the spirit that gives life, the flesh is of no avail; the words that I have spoken to you are spirit and life"* (Jn 62-63). *Many* disciples who know Jesus well now *"drew back and no longer went about with him"* (Jn 6:66). Many contemporary Christians who do not know of or do not accept the 2000-year-old Christian tradition of interpreting this passage believe that Jesus now says He was only speaking figuratively. It is clear that His disciples who know Him personally do not understand Him to be speaking figuratively. Many (Greek *polloi*, which means a great many, perhaps most of those present) of Jesus' disciples abandon Him. And Jesus lets them go. It is unconscionable that His disciples who have given up everything to follow Him, He would now let remain in misunderstanding of His teaching and so leave Him. A disciple reaches his fulfillment when understands everything from his Rabbi teaches and can teach it himself; that is what being a disciple means. Jesus always did this for His disciples; he even did it for timid Nicodemas. How could Jesus let His disciples go away, risking their salvation, based upon a misunderstanding.

It now seems as if only the twelve are left. Jesus turns to them. He does not explain to them that He was just speaking figuratively when He said His disciples have to "eat" (*trogo*) His flesh and drink His blood. He asks them if they will go away too. Peter as the head disciple responds for them all. He asks Jesus: "Lord to whom shall we go? (Jn 6:68). Peter doesn't say, we understand you were speaking figuratively. He doesn't ask the Lord to explain it in some other way. Like those disciples who walked away because of this difficult saying, Peter knows the Lord means it and that it is indeed a hard saying. Peter's response goes on to say that they know Jesus has the words of everlasting life, that He is the Holy One of God and so they choose to believe even though they know not how this will be. It is at this point that Jesus implies there is one of the twelve who does not believe, the one who is to betray Him Jesus calls a devil.

Now some suggest that the term "flesh and blood" is just a Hebrew idiom meaning the whole man. In other words, eating and drinking flesh and blood refers to the entirety of Jesus. This is true, but it is clearly not being used in that idiomatic sense here. We never see eating flesh and drinking blood when referring to the "whole man." However, there is a Palestinian idiom which uses the image of eating one's flesh and blood, but if that were used here it would lead to an untenable situation. To eat one's flesh and drink one's blood in ancient Palestine, as well as among Arabs today, meant to inflict serious harm on someone, especially by slander (see Jer 19:9, Ezek 39:4, 17-20, Rev 19:17, 18, 21 used to depict a curse). So Jesus would have been saying - "He that reviles me has eternal life" - a non-sensical command.

So what does Jesus mean by *"It is the Spirit that gives life, the flesh is of no avail;"*? Well in the context He is talking about His Resurrection and Ascension into heaven when He says, "Then what if you were to see the Son of man ascending where he was before?" He is clarifying for them that it will be after Pentecost and the coming of the Holy Spirit that this will be done. Only when the Holy Spirit comes will fallen flesh have access to everlasting life, through His flesh and blood. Fallen flesh alone cannot save itself; it will have to have access to His Risen flesh and blood. Again, it is obvious by the departure of *many* of His disciples after he said the spirit gives life, the response of Peter, and Jesus' words that no one present at the Bread of Life Discourse can be said to think that Jesus is saying He was only speaking figuratively.

Neither did the early Church take Jesus figuratively. St. Paul's first letter to the Corinthians is an important example of the literal understanding the Church has always applied to the Bread of the Life discourse. In this passage, Paul tells the Corinthians: *"For as often as you eat this bread and drink the cup, you proclaim the Lord's death until he comes. Whoever, therefore, eats the bread or drinks the cup of the Lord in an unworthy manner will be guilty of the body and blood of the Lord"* (1 Cor 11:26-27). The phrase "guilty of the Body and Blood" is a juridical phrase which carried the connotation of being guilty of murder. How can one be guilty of murder if St Paul is talking about anything other than the actual Body and Blood of Jesus. Paul goes on to say: *"Let a man examine himself, and so eat of the bread and drink of the cup. For anyone who eats and drinks without discerning the body eats and drinks judgment upon himself. That is why many of you are weak and ill, and some have died"* (1 Cor 11:28-30). It is obvious that for St. Paul, partaking of Jesus' body and blood in an unworthy manner is something to be considered with the utmost seriousness.

EARLY CHURCH FATHERS: REAL PRESENCE OF CHRIST IN THE EUCHARIST

St. Ignatius of Antioch

Those, indeed, who belong to God and to Jesus Christ—they are with the bishop. And those who repent and come to the unity of the Church—they too shall be of God, and will be living according to Jesus Christ. Do not err, my brethren: if anyone follow a schismatic, he will not inherit the Kingdom of God. If any man walk about with strange doctrine, he cannot lie down with the passion. Take care, then, to use one Eucharist, so that whatever you do, you do according to God: for there is one Flesh of our Lord Jesus Christ, and one cup in the union of His Blood; one altar, as there is one bishop with the presbytery and my fellow servants, the deacons.

Letter to the Philadelphians 7.3 (AD 110)

I have no taste for corruptible food nor for the pleasures of this life. I desire the Bread of God which is the Flesh of Jesus Christ, who was of the seed of David; and for drink I desire His Blood, which is love incorruptible.

Letter to the Romans 3.2, (AD 110)

He was a follower of St. John. He knew what St. John meant in his Gospel when he recounted Jesus' "Bread of Life" discourse. "Take note of those who hold heterodox opinions on the grace of Jesus Christ which has come to us, and see how contrary their opinions are to the mind of God.... They abstain from the Eucharist and from prayer, because they do not confess that the Eucharist is the Flesh of our Savior Jesus Christ, Flesh which suffered for our sins and which the Father in heaven raised up again."

Letter to the Smyrnaeans 6.2, (110 AD)

St. Justin Martyr

For not as common bread nor common drink do we receive these; but since Jesus Christ our Savior was made incarnate by the word of God and had both flesh and blood for our salvation, so too, as we have been taught, the food which has been made into the Eucharist by the Eucharistic prayer set down by Him, and by the change of which our blood and flesh is nourished, is the flesh and the blood of that incarnated Jesus.

First Apology 65, (AD 148-155)

St. Irenaeus of Lyon

They are vain in every respect, who despise the entire dispensation of God, and deny the salvation of the body and spurn its regeneration, saying that it is not capable of immortality. If the body be not saved, then, in fact, neither did the Lord redeem us with His Blood; and neither is the cup of the Eucharist the partaking of His Blood nor is the Bread which we break the partaking of His Body.... As we are His members, so too are we nourished by means of created things, He Himself granting us the creation, causing His sun to rise and sending rain as He wishes. He has declared the cup, a part of creation, to be His own Blood, from which He causes our blood to flow; and the bread, a part of creation, He has established as His own Body, from which He gives increase to our bodies. When, therefore, the mixed cup and the baked bread receives the Word of God and becomes the Eucharist, the Body of Christ, and from these the substance of our flesh is increased and supported, how can they say that the flesh is not capable of receiving the gift of God, which is eternal life—flesh which is nourished by the Body and Blood of the Lord, and is in fact a member of Him? In this regard the blessed Paul says in his Epistle to the Ephesians: "Because we are members of His Body, from His flesh and His bones." ...In the same way that the wood of the vine planted in the ground bears fruit in due season; or as a grain of wheat, falling on the ground, decomposes and rises up in manifold increase through the Spirit of God who contains all things; and then, through the Wisdom of God, comes to the service of men, and receiving the Word of God, becomes the Eucharist, which is the Body and Blood of Christ; so also our bodies, nourished by it, and deposited in the earth and decomposing therein, shall rise up in due season, the Word of God favoring them with resurrection in the glory of God the Father.

Against Heresies 4.18.4 (ca. AD 180/199)

Origen

I wish to admonish you with examples from your religion. You are accustomed to take part in the divine mysteries, so you know how, when you have received the Body of the Lord, you reverently exercise every care lest a particle of it fall, and lest anything of the consecrated gift perish. You account yourselves guilty, and rightly do you so believe, if any of it be lost through negligence. But if you observe such caution in keeping His Body, and properly so, how is it that you think neglecting the word of God a lesser crime than neglecting His Body?

Homilies on Exodus 13.3, (post AD 244)

St. Ephraim

Our Lord Jesus took in His hands what in the beginning was only bread; and He blessed it, and signed it, and made it holy in the name of the Father and in the name of the Spirit; and He broke it and in His gracious kindness He distributed it to all His disciples one by one. He called the bread His living Body, and did Himself fill it with Himself and the Spirit. And extending His hand, He gave them the Bread which His right hand had made holy: "Take, all of you eat of this, which My word has made holy. Do not now regard as bread that which I have given you; but take, eat this Bread, and do not scatter the crumbs; for what I have called My Body, that it is indeed. One particle from its crumbs is able to sanctify thousands and thousands, and is sufficient to afford life to those who eat of it. Take, eat, entertaining no doubt of faith, because this is My Body, and whoever eats it in belief eats in it Fire and Spirit. But if any doubter eat of it, for him it will be only bread. And whoever eats in belief the Bread made holy in My name, if he be pure, he will be preserved in his purity; and if he be a sinner, he will be forgiven." But if anyone despise it or reject it or treat it with ignominy, it may be taken as a certainty that he treats with ignominy the Son, who called it and actually made it to be His Body.

Homilies 4.4, (ca. AD 306-373)

St. Cyril of Jerusalem

[Our Lord Jesus Christ] Himself, therefore, having declared and said of the Bread, "This is My Body," who will dare any longer to doubt? And when He Himself has affirmed and said, "This is My Blood," who can ever hesitate and say it is not His Blood?

Catechetical Lectures 22(*Mystagogic* 4).1, (AD 350)

Do not, therefore, regard the Bread and the Wine as simply that; for they are, according to the Master's declaration, the Body and Blood of Christ. Even though the senses suggest to you the other, let faith make you firm. Do not judge in this matter by taste, but—be fully assured by the faith, not doubting that you have been deemed worthy of the Body and Blood of Christ.

Catechetical Lectures 22(*Mystagogic* 4).6, (AD 350)

Having learned these things, and being fully convinced that the apparent Bread is not bread, even though it is sensible to the taste, but the Body of Christ; and that the apparent Wine is not wine, even though the taste would have it so; and that of old David spoke of this, when he sang, "And bread strengthens the heart of man, so much so that his face is made cheerful with oil,"—strengthen your heart, partake of that Bread as something spiritual, and put a cheerful face on your soul.

Catechetical Lectures 22(*Mystagogic* 4).9, (AD 350)

St. Hilary of Poitiers

When we speak of the reality of Christ's nature being in us, we would be speaking foolishly and impiously—had we not learned it from Him. For He Himself says: "My Flesh is truly Food, and My Blood is truly Drink. He that eats My Flesh and drinks My Blood will remain in Me and I in him." As to the reality of His Flesh and Blood, there is no room left for doubt, because now, both by the declaration of the Lord Himself and by our own faith, it is truly Flesh and it is truly Blood. And These Elements bring it about, when taken and consumed, that we are in Christ and Christ is in us. Is this not true? Let those who deny that Jesus Christ is true God be free to find these things untrue. But He Himself is in us through the flesh and we are in Him, while that which we are with Him is in God.

On the Trinity 8.14, (ca. AD 356-359)

St. Gregory of Nyssa

He offered Himself for us, Victim and Sacrifice, and Priest as well, and "Lamb of God, who takes away the sin of the world." When did He do this? When He made His own Body food and His own Blood drink for His disciples; for this much is clear enough to anyone, that a sheep cannot be eaten by a man unless its being eaten be preceded by its being slaughtered. This giving of His own Body to His disciples for eating clearly indicates that the sacrifice of the Lamb has now been completed.

Sermon One: On the Resurrection of Christ (Jaeger 9.287), (ca. AD 335-394)

St. John Chrysostom

"The cup of blessing which we bless, is it not communion of the Blood of Christ?" Very trustworthily and awesomely does he say it. For what he is saying is this: "What is in the cup is that which flowed from His side, and we partake of it." He called it a cup of blessing because when we hold it in our hands that is how we praise Him in song, wondering and astonished at His indescribable Gift, blessing Him because of His having poured out this very Gift so that we might not remain in error; and not only for His having poured It out, but also for His sharing It with all of us. "If therefore you desire blood," He says, "do not redden the platform of idols with the slaughter of dumb beasts, but My altar of sacrifice with My Blood." What is more awesome than this? What, pray tell, more tenderly loving?

Homilies on the First Letter to the Corinthians 24.1(3), (ca AD 392)

"Because the Bread is one, we, the many, are in one Body." "Why do I say 'communion?' " he says; "for we are that very Body." What is the Bread? The Body of Christ! What do they become who are partakers therein? The Body of Christ! Not many bodies, but one Body. For just as the bread, consisting of many grains, is made one, and the grains are no longer evident, but still exist, though their distinction is not apparent in their conjunction; so too are we conjoined to each other and to Christ. For you are not nourished by one Body while someone else is nourished by another Body; rather, all are nourished by the same Body.

Homilies on the First Letter to the Corinthians 24.2(4), (ca AD 392)

When you see [the Body of Christ] lying on the altar, say to yourself, "Because of this Body I am no longer earth and ash, no longer a prisoner, but free. Because of this Body I hope for heaven, and I hope to receive the good things that are in heaven, immortal life, the lot of the angels, familiar conversation with Christ. This Body, scourged and crucified, has not been fetched by death.... This is that Body which was blood-stained, which was pierced by a lance, and from which gushed forth those saving fountains, one of blood and the other of water, for all the world." ...This is the Body which He gave us, both to hold in reserve and to eat, which was appropriate to intense love; for those whom we kiss with abandon we often even bite with our teeth.

Homilies on the First Letter to the Corinthians 24.4(7), (ca AD 392)

Theodore of Mopsuestia

It is proper therefore, that when [Christ] gave the Bread He did not say, "This is the symbol of My Body," but, "This is My Body." In the same way when He gave the Cup He did not say, "This is the symbol of My Blood," but, "This is My Blood"; for He wanted us to look upon the [Eucharistic elements] after their reception of grace and the coming of the Holy Spirit not according to their nature, but [that we should] receive them as they are, the Body and

Blood of our Lord. We ought ...not regard the [Eucharistic elements] merely as bread and cup, but as the Body and Blood of Christ, into which they were transformed by the descent of the Holy Spirit.

Catechetical Homilies 5, (+ AD 428)

St. Ambrose of Milan

Perhaps you may be saying: I see something else; how can you assure me that I am receiving the Body of Christ? It but remains for us to prove it. And how many are the examples we might use! Let us prove that this is not what nature has shaped it to be, but what the blessing has consecrated; for the power of the blessing is greater than that of nature, because by the blessing even nature itself is changed.

The Mysteries 9.50, (AD 390-391)

Christ is in that Sacrament, because it is the Body of Christ; yet, it is not on that account corporeal food, but spiritual. Whence also His Apostle says of the type: "For our fathers ate spiritual food and drank spiritual drink." For the body of God is a spiritual body.

The Mysteries 9.58, (AD 390-391)

St. Augustine of Hippo

I am mindful of my promise. For I promised you, who have now been baptized, a sermon in which I would explain the Sacrament of the Lord's Table, which you now look upon and of which you last night were made participants. You ought to know what you have received, what you are going to receive, and what you ought to receive daily. That Bread which you see on the altar, having been sanctified by the word of God, is the Body of Christ. That chalice, or rather, what is in that chalice, having been sanctified by the word of God, is the Blood of Christ. Through that bread and wine the Lord Christ willed to commend His Body and Blood, which He poured out for us unto the forgiveness of sins. If you have received worthily, you are what you have received. For the Apostle says: "Because the Bread is one, we, though many, are one body. Thus he explained the Sacrament of the Lord's Table: "Because the Bread is one, we, though many, are one body." Thus, by that Bread, you are taught how you must love unity. For is that bread made of but one grain of wheat? Were there not in fact many grains? But before they became bread, they were separate; by water they were joined together, and that was after a certain *contrition.*

Sermon 227, (ca. AD 391-430)

What you see is the bread and the chalice; that is what your own eyes report to you. But what your faith obliges you to accept is that the bread is the Body of Christ and the chalice the Blood of Christ. This has been said very briefly, which may perhaps be sufficient for faith; yet faith does desire instruction.... How is the bread His Body? And the chalice, or what is in the chalice, how is it His Blood? Those elements, brethren, are called Sacraments, because in them one thing is seen, but another is understood. What is seen is the corporeal species; but what is understood is the spiritual fruit. If, then, you wish to understand the Body of Christ, hear the Apostle speaking to the faithful: "You, however, are the Body of

Christ and His members. If, therefore, you are the Body of Christ and His members, your mystery is presented at the table of the Lord: you receive your mystery. To that which you are, you answer: "Amen"; and by answering, you subscribe to it. For you hear: "The Body of Christ!" and you answer: "Amen!" Be a member of Christ's Body, so that your "Amen" may be the truth.

Sermon 272, (ca. AD 391-430)

St. Leo the Great

When the Lord says: "Unless you shall have eaten the flesh of the Son of Man and shall have drunk His blood, you shall not have life in you," you ought to so communicate at the Sacred Table that you have no doubt whatever of the truth of the Body and Blood of Christ. For that which is taken in the mouth is what is believed in faith; and in vain do those respond, "Amen," who argue against that which is received.

Sermons 91.3, (before AD 461)

NOTES

SESSION 12: THE SACRAMENTS OF HEALING – RECONCILIATION & ANOINTING OF THE SICK

READING ASSIGNMENT

Page 56: questions 200-201; pages 87-92: questions 295-320

STUDY QUESTIONS

Reconciliation:

- If God loves me how I am, why must I repent and change my life? (CCCC qq: 295-298)
- What will it require of me to repent from my sinful attachments and commit to change my life? (CCCC qq: 299, 301, 303)
- Can I see authentic freedom in being freed from slavery to my previous sinful choices? (CCCC qq: 300, 303, 310)
- What does it mean to receive God's forgiveness through the mediation of a man? (CCCC q: 307)

Anointing of the Sick:

- Can I see the connection between the illness of the body and the sickness of the soul? (CCCC qq: 313, 315, 319)

NOTES:

TUTORIAL ON THE SACRAMENTS OF HEALING

Sacrament of Penance: Reconciliation with the Lord

This Sacrament is called by several names, each of which suggests a different aspect of the Sacrament: the Sacrament of Penance, Confession, Reconciliation, forgiveness, and conversion. Christ instituted it because even after Baptism, where we are made perfectly holy, we still have concupiscence and temptation from the devil. We can and do continue to fall into sin and need sanctifying grace to strengthen us for conversion and to restore us to communion when it is lost.

Conversion is the prerequisite, not only for becoming a Christian, but also for being a Christian . . . that is, for authentically living the life of a Christian. Conversion is obligatory in order to be baptized, but it does not end with Baptism. A life of continuing conversion is necessary for every Christian. Conversion requires outward acts as well as interior repentance. Outward acts express and at the same time bring about and deepen interior repentance. Conversion and repentance are authentic to the degree they bring about a radical reorientation of one's entire life.

All acts of interior penance revolve around the acts of religion: prayer, fasting and almsgiving. They are acts of religion because they express what it means to completely turn away from sin and to give oneself to God. Living these acts of religion in one's life involves ongoing daily conversion through acts of self-giving love and self-denial.

The Eucharist is the source and summit of Christian life and so it is the center of a life of conversion, penance, and self-denial. A deep life of prayer, especially enriched by reading and meditation on Scripture, is the place in which all other acts of religion come together and bear their fruit. Interior penance is also fruitfully developed by an intentional encounter with the mysteries of Christ's life expressed throughout the liturgical year's penitential days and seasons: Fridays, Pre-lent /Lent and Advent.

The Sacrament of Penance and Reconciliation is best viewed from a realistic understanding of sin. Sin is at root a rebellion against God; it is putting one's own will over against God's will. It is nothing less than a purposeful (in various degrees of intentionality) offense against God, and so it is one's willful alienation from Him. In the case of mortal sin, when the matter is grave, the knowledge is full and the consent is complete, it is one's willful, complete rupture of communion with Him. The Church itself *is* communion with Jesus Christ and so union with the Church is man's communion with God. Therefore, damage to one's relationship with God results in the same damage to one's communion with His Church and vice versa. Therefore, a new act of reconciliation with God and His Church is required when we sin gravely, and this is the purpose of the Sacrament.

Our reconciliation is an act of God, brought about liturgically in His Church by which He first invites the sinner to repentance and conversion, and then provides the means to accept this invitation through His Church's ministers. The Church does this through the office Jesus Christ established with Peter and His Apostles by which they are given the authority and power to "bind and loose" (see Mt 16:19; 18:18). The Sacrament of Reconciliation then has these two elements: 1) man's interior conversion by responding to the action of the Holy Spirit, 2) God's action through the Church's intervention.

Valid "form" and "matter" are necessary for the validity of Sacramental Confession. The essential form is when the priest (or bishop) says the words of absolution: *"God, the Father of mercies, through the death and the resurrection of his Son has reconciled the world to himself and sent the Holy Spirit among us for the forgiveness of sins; through the ministry of the Church may God give you pardon and peace, and I absolve you from your sins in the name of the Father, and of the Son, and of the Holy Spirit"* (CCC 1449). The valid matter includes authentic contrition and confession of the penitent, and acts of satisfaction by him.

Contrition is *"sorrow of the soul and detestation for the sin committed, together with the resolution not to sin again"* (CCC 1451). There is "perfect contrition," which occurs when the penitent is contrite due to his love for God above all else; this is a gift of actual grace from God. Perfect contrition remits venial sins and obtains forgiveness of mortal sins, if the penitent has the firm commitment of going to the Sacrament of Confession as soon as possible. There is also "imperfect contrition" (also called attrition), which is also a gift from God, but arises from one's revulsion of the ugliness of sin and/or fear of everlasting damnation and other punishments due to sin. This prompts one to go to Confession where the penitent receives Sacramental absolution.

Examination of conscience is necessary before one goes to Confession. This examination is a systematic review of one's life and evaluating it against the Ten Commandments and Beatitudes as described in the Church's moral teaching. Such examination is a necessary practice for a fruitful life of ongoing conversion, and to be fruitful it is highly recommended by spiritual masters to be a nightly exercise. After determining one's sins through the examination, one must then confess his sins to a priest in his presence (absolution is not valid if confession and absolution are not done in the physical presence of the priest). Confession is obligatory for the forgiveness of all mortal sins and highly recommended for venial sins. The habitual nature of which can lead one to commit mortal sin. Confession to the priest is where one receives absolution as we described above in discussing the form of the Sacrament.

Satisfaction describes the acts of love and reparation the penitent makes to repair the damage to oneself, to other members of the Church and to the world done by one's sins. Absolution takes away sin, but it does not repair the damage done. Justice and love for God and others demands one undertake the task of making reparations. Reparation begins with the penance given by the priest in Confession but continues through one's ongoing acts of religion (prayer, fasting, almsgiving) he offers in reparation throughout his life.

There are only two valid ministers of the Sacrament of Confession: a validly ordained bishop or priest (only Catholic, Orthodox and Oriental Christian bishops and priests have valid Holy Orders). Confession to anyone else is not a valid Sacramental Confession. The fruits of the Sacrament of Confession are reconciliation with God, with the Church and all its members, with oneself, and with the rest of creation.

Indulgences are gifts of God through His Church which bring about the remission of "the temporal punishment due to sin" (CCC 1471). This temporal punishment due to sin is at root suffering and dying to self and offering this suffering for reparations for our sins through acts of love and religion. Reparational suffering is necessary to repair the damage our sins have caused and to purify us so as to be ready to meet God face to face in heaven. Until we have had the opportunity to cooperate in complete reparation for all of our sins, we have not finished learning to love adequately.

Indulgences are the treasury of the Church, the Head and Body of Christ, that He and His saints have offered for sin that can be applied on behalf of every member of the Church to repair the damage done to oneself, the Church, and the world by one's sins. Indulgences are either plenary (which remit all temporal punishment) or partial (because they repair only part of the damage done). To obtain an indulgence, the Pope proposes specific time frames and acts (e.g., specific prayers said during a pilgrimage to certain churches during a year dedicated to a particular intention).

The general requirements to obtain an indulgence include: going to Confession and Holy Communion within about 20 days before or after one undertakes the particular observance. In addition, one must be in a state of grace, have the interior disposition of complete detachment from every sin (even venial sins), and pray for the Pope's intentions. One may do the act once per day to gain separate indulgences. One Sacramental Confession suffices for several indulgences within the required time frame, but a separate reception of Holy Communion and prayers for the Pope's intentions are required for each indulgence. Indulgences can be applied to oneself or to the souls of the deceased in purgatory.

Sacrament of Anointing of the Sick

Illness and suffering challenges us in ways almost nothing else can. If we permit, it can show us our complete dependence upon God and open us to His invitation to faith and hope. If we refuse its lessons, it can lead us to a bitter rejection of God and to despair. In the Old Testament, illness and suffering were connected with sin. They were often associated with punishment from God for specific sins. The truth is that suffering, illness, and death do enter the world through sin, but the innocent and guilty alike suffer from them because of creation's estrangement from God which comes with the fall of Adam and Eve. In the New Testament, Jesus reveals that He comes to save man integrally, that is, body and soul. Of course, the soul has priority. Jesus shows a special concern for the sick and suffering.

Jesus' solicitude for the sick and suffering is carried on in His Church. Jesus comes to the ill Christian in a special way, in the Sacrament of the Anointing of the Sick. We see this Sacrament manifested in the Letter of St. James, in which he says if a Christian is ill to call for the presbyters (priests) who will pray for and anoint the sick person. The prayers and anointing of the priest will save him and if he has sinned, his sins will be forgiven (see James 5:13-15). Mark's Gospel also mentions this Sacrament in the healing of the sick through anointing (see Mark 6:13).

Anointing of the Sick used to be called extreme unction (which means "final anointing") because it was primarily given as part of the last rites one received before dying. It still is, but today we call it the Sacrament of the Sick because it is intended that Catholics receive it when illness, the ravages of old age or even surgery make death a possibility. In some circumstances, a non-Catholic Christian may receive it. However, he must ask for it of his own volition and demonstrate that he believes what the Catholic Church teaches about the Sacrament.

Only a validly ordained bishop or priest has the power to administer this Sacrament. The Church teaches that laity should not ask for and priests should not bless "holy oils" for lay use as sacramentals as this leads to confusion about the Sacrament of Anointing. Only the Oil of the Infirm, blessed by the bishop at the Chrism Mass on Holy Thursday (which for the sake of logistics is often celebrated before Holy Week in some spread out dioceses) is to be used, except in cases of extreme emergency (when the priest can bless olive oil only for that anointing).

Anointing of the Sick provides the fruits of strength, peace and fortitude with which to face the pilgrimage of the Cross to which God calls the sick and aged. It brings the recipient into a more intimate communion with Christ's Passion, providing him with strength and peace. It also prepares him for his final journey, should this particular journey lead to death. It is intended to form a three-fold set of last rites, which is composed of Confession, Anointing of the Sick and Viaticum (the final reception of Holy Communion). The "form" of the Sacrament is the words of epiclesis the priest says in calling down the Holy Spirit upon the sick person and the "matter" is the anointing with the Oil of the Infirm.

PREPARING FOR AND GOING TO CONFESSION

"In the Church, there are two conversions, water, and tears: the water of Baptism, and the tears of repentance."   - St. Ambrose, Bishop of Milan (d. 397)

Requirements for Authentic Reconciliation

The following five steps comprise the procedure for a Catholic to encounter Jesus Christ in an authentic and healing manner, in the Sacrament of Penance (i.e., for a valid Confession). If one skips or performs any of these steps inadequately, the fruitfulness of the Sacrament can be diminished or it can even be invalid (e.g., if one does not intend to stop performing a particular sin, God does not forgive one's sins). The five steps are:

1. **Examination of conscience:** Before going to confession, you must recollect your life since your last confession. The purpose for this is to take account of the way one is living his life, the sins of which he is guilty, and any sinful patterns to which he has become enslaved. This assessment can be made much easier and more effective by doing a nightly examination of conscience. This recollection is an evaluation of sins of commission (evil acts taken) and sins of omission (actions one had a moral obligation to perform but failed to do so) for which one is culpable. It can be helpful to use a previously prepared examination of conscience aid to assist you. There are many good examinations of conscience aids available. We provide a simple guide below.

2. **Sincere contrition for sins:** Contrition is being sorry for one's sins for which he is culpable. Contrition can be motivated by fear of the consequences (i.e., fear of hell), which is called imperfect contrition or by love for God and sorrow for offending Him (called perfect contrition). Imperfect contrition can be a starting point for repentance but forgiveness requires sincere sorrow rather than simply fear of the consequences. It is important to realize that contrition is not a matter of feelings but it is a choice one freely makes. One can be sincerely contrite without experiencing feelings of guilt, shame or sorrow. An inability to feel guilt or sorrow suggests a lack of self-mastery which needs to be addressed, but it does not invalidate confession. Living a life of virtue and love, and praying to God for the full experience of one's sorrow can help you to overcome the lack of emotions associated with repentance.

3. **Make a firm purpose of amendment:** It is necessary to firmly commit yourself to not performing the sin(s) you are confessing again, and to avoid all occasions that make the sin(s) more likely. However, it is important to realize that there is a difference between the commitment to amending one's life and the realization that some patterns of behavior will take time to change. For example, addictions can make one less culpable for certain sinful behaviors. An alcoholic who has made the decision to repent, also should understand that he may not be able to avoid getting drunk right away because of his alcoholism. However, he can still commit to not getting drunk again and receive forgiveness. On the other, someone who, say, regularly engages in

148

sex outside of marriage cannot go to confession and receive absolution if his intention is to continue the same sinful behavior. One should seek counsel from a priest on any questions he may have about his circumstance, and for guidance on overcoming any sins to which he may be enslaved.

4. **Confess your sins:** One must go to the Sacrament of Confession (either at the appointed times or by appointment) and confess your sins to a Catholic priest in order to receive absolution (see the suggested procedure below). At Our Lady of the Atonement, the confessionals have the penitent behind a screen. However, at most other parishes one may go to, there will usually also be an option to go to confession face to face with the priest. If the face-to-face option is available, it is still your choice which method you prefer to use.

5. **Perform the assigned penance:** The priest will assign some specific penance for you to accomplish. This is usually saying certain prayers, some other act(s) of devotion, and/or some act(s) of reparation when appropriate. One should perform these actions as soon as possible after leaving the confessional. If the penance is, for example, three Hail Mary's, it would be advisable to go directly to a pew in the church and say these prayers.

Examination of Conscience

The following is a brief examination of conscience based upon the Ten Commandments:

1. *I am the Lord your God. You shall not have strange gods before me.*
   Have I failed to love God adequately? Have I omitted daily prayers? Have I consented to temptations to doubt or to deny the Catholic faith? Have I tempted my faith by reading or listening to material against the Catholic faith? Have I sinned against God and against my trust in Him by choosing to follow superstitious practices (e.g., New Age practices, Scientology, astrology, horoscopes, fortune-telling, meditative yoga (or any other meditation in which you open yourself to anything spiritual, etc.)? Have I consulted demons in a misguided attempt for personal gain through Occult practices (e.g., use of the Ouija board, consulting so-called witches/asking for spells, going to a palm reader/fortune teller, engaging in satanic ceremonies, etc.)? Did I endanger my Catholic faith or cause scandal by associating with anti-Catholic groups & associations (e.g., New Age groups, Freemasons, atheist organizations, agnostic/freethinking organizations, etc.)? Have I permitted fame, fortune, money, career, pleasure, etc. to replace God as my highest priority in life?

2. *You shall not take the name of the Lord your God in vain.*
   Have I used God's name in vain by lightly, carelessly, or blasphemously invoking His name (as these names are to be used only to praise)? Have I cursed or sworn through the use of profane language and so diminished the dignity of other persons

or myself? Have I insulted anyone's God-given name? Have I committed sacrilege by showing disrespect to holy objects (e.g., a crucifix, the rosary, a blessed statue, etc.) or contempt for religious persons (bishops, priests, deacons, women religious) or for sacred places (a church or blessed shrine). Have I committed sacrilege by going to Holy Communion in the state of mortal sin without first going to confession? Have I purposefully or carelessly violated the one-hour fast before Communion? Did I break the laws of fast and abstinence during Lent and the rest of the year? Have I neglected to support the Church and the poor by sharing the gifts God has given me (time, abilities, money)?

3. ***Remember to keep holy the Lord's Day.***
   Have I missed Mass through my own fault and without a serious reason on Sundays or Holy Days of Obligation? Was I late for Mass or did I leave before the Mass was proclaimed to be ended without a good reason? Did I permit my children who have reached the age of reason to miss Mass without a good reason? Did I neglect my Easter duty or my yearly Confession duty? Do I do unnecessary, servile work on Sunday (by which I am showing I do not trust in God and His Providence)? Do I consent to being distracted at Mass (e.g., in order to make the time seem to go by more quickly) and so fail to participate?

4. ***Honor your father and your mother.***
   Do you honor your parents by being thankful and respectful to them? If you are under 18 and still living with them, have you obeyed them? If they are in old age and you have the means, do you visit them, and/or assist them with their needs for which they can no longer provide for themselves? Have you obeyed others with lawful authority over you in the Church and civilly? As parents, have you neglected your children's religious education, taught them to pray and led them in prayer, taught them virtue and morality, set a good Christian example for them, and ensured they attend Mass? For married people, have you separated or divorced civilly without getting permission from the Bishop?

5. ***You shall not kill.***
   Have I been mean or unjust to anyone? Do I complain more than I compliment? Am I ungrateful for what other people do for me? Have I committed calumny (lying or spreading rumors which damages another's reputation) or detraction (telling a truth about someone without a serious reason and which damages his reputation)? Do I tear people down rather than encourage them? Have I failed to correct others with kindness? Have I judged someone's soul as damned by God or wished them damned? Do I point out others' faults and mistakes while ignoring my own? Have I consented to deep anger, resentment, or hatred for another person? Have I fought with another person unjustly? Have I held a grudge or sought revenge against someone who wronged me? Have I given bad example or scandal (i.e., led another

person to believe a sinful act is ok)? Have I freely given up control over my faculties to know the truth and to act on the truth through drunkenness or illicit drugs? Have I endangered the lives of others by reckless driving or by driving under the influence of drugs or alcohol? Do I show contempt for my body by neglecting to take care of my own health? Am I prejudiced against people because of their skin color, language, or ethnic-religious background? Have I procured, helped obtain, approved of, permitted or encouraged an abortion? Have I procured, helped obtain, permitted or encouraged the sterilization of another person (vasectomy, tubal ligation, etc.) to avoid children? Have I actively or passively cooperated with an act of euthanasia whereby ordinary medical means were withdrawn or active means taken to directly end the life of any person? Have I committed an act of violence or abuse (physical, sexual, emotional, or verbal)? Have I killed someone or helped to kill, permitted the killing of, or encouraged the killing of another human being?

6. *You shall not commit adultery.*

Have I consented to any impure sexual thoughts? Have I engaged in any unchaste or impure sexual acts with another (e.g., passionate kisses, sinful touches, etc. with someone with whom I am not married)? Have I engaged in thoughts or acts that have led to impure or unchaste acts with another person? Have I dressed or behaved immodestly or in a way intended to sexually excite another person? Have I read or viewed pornography: on the internet, in impure books, magazines, videos, etc.)? Do I needlessly and/or carelessly subject myself to impurity or pornography in the television shows, by internet habits, movies, etc. that I watch, without using available guides that warn me beforehand? Have I engaged in fornication (pre-marital sex)? Have I committed adultery (marital infidelity)? Have I used or permitted the use of birth control (by pill, devices, withdrawal)? Do I avoid all occasions of impurity? Do I view pornographic material (magazines, videos, internet, hot lines)? Have I not avoided the occasions of sin (persons or places) which would tempt me to be unfaithful to my spouse or to my own chastity? Do I encourage and entertain impure thoughts and desires? Do I tell or listen to impure jokes, stories, or other such conversations?

7. *You shall not steal.*

Have I taken something that does not belong to me without the permission of the owner? Have I cheated anyone of their money or possessions? Do I steal habitually? Have I been late, left early, or wasted time at work without the permission of my supervisor? Do I neglect my responsibilities to do my best in school or in my responsibilities at home? Have I cheated on exams or taken others' work as my own? Am I stingy with the gifts God has given me? Do I gamble excessively? Have I neglected to pay my debts or taxes promptly? Do I live sufficiently in poverty of spirit and detachment? Have I supported my parish regularly and given to charity? Have I been stingy in my support for the Church? Do I give back to God the time & abilities He has given me? Have I knowingly deceived someone in business or committed fraud? Have I shown disrespect or even contempt for another's property? Have I committed any acts of vandalism? Have I been habitually lazy or idle and neglected my responsibilities to God and others?

8. *You shall not bear false witness against your neighbor.*

Have I lied in order to deceive someone? Have I gossiped about someone? Do I always tell the truth? Have I talked about another person behind his back? Have I revealed secrets that should have been kept secret? Have I been critical, negative, or uncharitable in my conversations? Have I committed perjury by falsely swearing an oath? Am I a busybody or do I love to spread gossip and secrets about others? Am I eager to hear bad news about others?

9. *You shall not covet your neighbor's wife.*

Have I consented to impure thoughts? Did I cause impure thoughts by stares, illicit reading, excessive curiosity, or impure conversations? Do I neglect to control my imagination? Did I pray at once to banish such bad thoughts and temptations? Did I consent to impure glances? Do I regularly practice custody of the eyes, thoughts, and emotions?

10. *You shall not covet your neighbor's goods.*

Have I consented to greedy temptations? Have I consented to jealousy or to envy of what another has? Do I ask God to keep me focused on being thankful for all the gifts He has given me? Do I let financial and material concerns or the desire for comfort override my duty to God, to Church, to my family or to my own spiritual well-being? Do I resist temptations to being negative or resentful because of what I do not have? Do I set my focus on earthly possessions or do I accept thankfully what I have on earth but set my heart on the good of others and eternal life with God?

PROCEDURE IN THE CONFESSIONAL

1. Enter the confessional and kneel facing the screen (in parishes other than Atonement, you will usually have the option to sit facing the priest or to kneel behind the screen).

2. Make the sign of the Cross (the priest should direct you, if not do it yourself) as you say: ***"Bless me Father for I have sinned. It has been _____ since my last confession (or "this is my first confession). Since then I have _____"***
    Tell all your mortal sins, the number of times, and any necessary circumstances (for example, for any sexual sins, tell him if you are married or single). You should also confess those venial sins that are current obstacles to your growth in holiness.

3. When finished, say: ***"That is all Father; I am truly sorry for these sins and for those which I may be forgetting to mention."***

4. The priest may then provide advice; he will assign your penance, after which you should indicate your acceptance of it, by saying: **"Yes, Father."**

5. The priest should direct you to say an Act of Contrition (if not, say this quietly during absolution): ***"O my God! I am heartily sorry for having offended Thee and I detest all my sins because of Thy just punishment, but most of all, because they have offended Thee, my God, Who art all good and deserving of all my love. I firmly resolve, with the help of Thy grace, to sin no more and to avoid the near occasion of sin. Amen."***

6. Listen closely as the priest gives you absolution; he will say: *"God, the Father of mercies, through the death and resurrection of his Son has reconciled the world to himself and sent the Holy Spirit among us for the forgiveness of sins; through the ministry of the Church may God give you pardon and peace, and I absolve you from your sins in the name of the Father, and of the Son, + and of the Holy Spirit."*

7. As he says the name of the Trinity, you should make the sign of the Cross and after he concludes, you say: **"Amen."**

8. The priest will then say: *"Give thanks to the Lord, for He is good."* You should then respond: **"For His mercy endures forever."**

9. Then the priest dismisses you, saying: *"The Lord has freed you from your sins. Go in peace."* And you may respond with: **"Thanks be to God."**

NOTES

SESSION 13: THE SACRAMENTS OF SERVICE – HOLY ORDERS & MATRIMONY

READING ASSIGNMENT

Pages 92-98: questions 321-350

STUDY QUESTIONS

Holy Orders:

- What does it mean that a priest acts in the person of Christ? (CCCC qq: 325, 326, 328)
- Can I see the love of Christ in the gift of the priesthood? (CCCC qq: 324, 329, 330, 334, 336)

Matrimony:

- What does it mean that God calls man into a covenant of marriage? (CCCC qq: 337, 338, 347, 350)
- How does marriage as a Sacrament in the Service of Communion and Mission ordered to the salvation of spouses, change the way I look at the meaning of marriage and all relationships? (CCCC qq: 339, 341, 346)

NOTES:

TUTORIAL ON SACRAMENTS IN THE SERVICE OF COMMUNION AND MISSION

The Sacraments in the Service of Communion and Mission, as they are called in the *Compendium to the Catechism of the Catholic Church*, is an apt description. These Sacraments are in the service of communion because they bring new members into the Body of Christ, and they reconcile and nurture the members of the Body. They are in the service of mission because they prepare and enable the members of the Body to go out with Christ to the far reaches of the world to bring the Good News of redemption to those who do not yet know Him in a saving manner. The Catechism itself uses the shorter name Sacraments of Service, so for the sake of economy we will use this shorter title.

The Sacraments of Service are unique among the Sacraments. The five other Sacraments are ordered directly to the justification and sanctification of the recipient. The two Sacraments of Service are ordered to making the recipient an effective mediator of salvation to others. These two Sacraments directly contribute to others' salvation but only indirectly to the salvation of the person receiving the Sacrament of Service.

The Sacraments of Service provide a particular consecration. The consecration to the common priesthood (also called the baptismal priesthood) comes through Baptism and Confirmation. The Sacraments of Service comprise two different consecrations, each of which transform the recipient to serve others in a particular way.

Holy Orders consecrates the recipient to the ministerial priesthood of Christ the Head in such a way that the recipient becomes a mediator of Christ in Word and Sacraments. In the degrees of priest and bishop, he is consecrated *in Persona Christi Capitis*. Marriage consecrates the recipients to a unique participation in the baptismal priesthood. It prepares and strengthens the spouses to serve one another and makes them to become mediators of sacramental grace to one another within the domestic church, the family.

The Sacrament of Holy Orders

Holy Orders is the ministry of the Apostles. It was instituted by Jesus Christ in order to exercise His ministry through the successors of the Apostles until the end of time; therefore, it is the Sacrament of Apostolic Succession or the Sacrament of Apostolic Ministry.

The priesthood of the Old Covenant becomes explicit only in the aftermath of Israel's rebellion in their worship of the golden calf during the 40 years wandering in the wilderness after their escape from Egyptian captivity. In the wake of this rebellion, the tribe of Levi is chosen to lead God's chosen people in the requirements of the covenant that God renews with Israel under Moses' leadership. However, the covenant between

Israel and God continues to be powerless to bring about the salvation of man, a salvation that has been needed since the fall of Adam and Eve.

Nevertheless, there are hints that the Old Covenant priesthood existed since Adam in the order of the firstborn son of each family, but which was given to the Levites due to their failure as priests (see e.g., Numbers 8:16). Jesus Christ has returned this primogeniture (firstborn) priesthood to Himself. His is the one High Priesthood that is different than that of the Levites, it is a priesthood after the order of Melchizedek. The complex and repetitious sacrificial system of the Mosaic Covenant overseen by the Levitical priesthood symbolized reconciliation but could not bring it about. Jesus' Sacrifice of the Cross is made once, for all time and for all men. This sacrifice is made present in the Holy Sacrifice of the Mass. Only Christ's Sacrifice has the power to reconcile man with God.

The ministerial priesthood is the priesthood of Christ the Head, which is different in essence not just degree, from the common priesthood of all the baptized. This hierarchical priesthood is for the sake of service to Christ and His Body, the members of His Church. As Christ offers His Sacrifice in the name of His Body to His Father, the ministerial priesthood in the Person of Christ acts in the name of the Church and on its behalf. However, it is essential to understand that priests are configured to Christ and receive their delegation from Him, not from the community. Christ gives His authority to the hierarchical priesthood to serve His Body, the Church but He does not give His Body authority over Him or His delegates, the hierarchal priesthood.

There are three degrees in this Sacrament. The highest is the episcopate (bishops), next is the presbyterate (priests), finally the lowest degree is the diaconate (deacons). Bishops and priests participate in mediating the Sacrifice of the Cross in the Mass, but Deacons do not. Therefore, the terms *sacerdos* (Latin for priest and implying the offering of sacrifice) and *in Persona Christi* are not applied to deacons.

In the degree of the episcopate, bishops have the fullness of Holy Orders. It is through bishops alone that apostolic succession is maintained, forming an unbroken line of succession back to Christ. If someone claiming to be a bishop is not validly ordained, he does not have apostolic succession and so is not in reality a bishop. Bishops have the fullness of the *tri-munera*, the threefold ministry of Christ's priesthood as priest, prophet, and king in his local church. The pope has this *tri-munera* over the universal Church. As priest, bishops have the authority to sanctify the people through the Sacraments. As prophet they have the unique authority to teach in Christ's name, which includes the obligation to guard the purity of the faith and to correct the faithful when necessary. As king, bishops have the authority to govern Christ's Body, the Church. The Pope has the authority over the universal Church on earth and each bishop has an analogous authority over the local church to which he is appointed.

The degree of the presbyterate is best understood as the bishops' co-workers in the parish. Just as bishops are the presence of Christ to the local church, priests are the presence of the bishop in the parish. Because priests function as their bishop's presence in the parish, they have the powers to act *in Persona Christi Capitis*. The priest depends upon his bishop for his authority to exercise his powers of priest/prophet/king in the parish.

The lowest degree of Holy Orders in the diaconate exists "in order to serve." Deacons are dedicated to serving the people on behalf of the bishop in his ministry of love to his flock. The deacon's tasks include assisting the bishop and priests in the liturgy, especially the Eucharist, but also assisting at marriages, proclaiming the Gospel, presiding over funerals, and being dedicated to other ministries of love. There are transitional deacons who are in the last step of their formation for the priesthood, and permanent deacons who are formed and ordained for the permanent vocation to assist the bishop in the diaconate.

The only valid minister of the Sacrament of Holy Orders is a validly ordained bishop. Those who may validly receive Holy Orders are baptized men only (males, Latin: *viri*). Jesus chose only men, and His Apostles followed this pattern (because of the meaning of the office as spiritual father). The Church understands that she is bound by Jesus' choice. The ordination of women, therefore, is simply not possible. The Sacrament is not a right, and no one is denied the grace necessary for salvation and sanctification because he is not eligible for this Sacrament. Celibacy is a requirement for a Latin Rite bishops and priests, as they are called to Holy Orders "for the sake of the kingdom of heaven" (Mt 19:12). In the Eastern Church, married men are permitted to be ordained as priests but not as bishops. No one ordained in either Rite (bishop, priest or deacon) may marry once he is ordained.

The effects of the Sacrament of Holy Orders include an indelible character. A new power is permanently infused in his soul, he will never be a layman again. The principle of ex *opere operato* (CCC 1584) means that the unworthiness minister doesn't prevent Christ from acting in the Sacraments.

The Sacrament of Matrimony

Marriage is more than a contract; it is a covenant. A covenant is an institution that forms a family relationship where there is not a previously existing family by nature. Therefore, a covenant is a life-long commitment to faithful, fruitful, exclusive, irrevocable, self-giving love. Marriage characterizes covenant love that is expressed in a sexually complementary, life-long commitment to the mutual flourishing of one another and to an openness to bearing and raising children. Spousal love is a unique form of love that is an inextricably union of mutual lifelong commitment to the integral good of one another and to the bringing forth of new persons. God has imbued this unified vocation with a character that includes exclusivity and fidelity in sexually complementary love that can be found and expressed in no other relationship. In Christian marriage, spousal love is transformed into redemptive love because of its incorporation to the relationship between Christ and the Church (see Eph 5:32).

God has woven marriage into and throughout the order of creation and His providential plan for it. The Canon of Sacred Scripture begins and ends with marriage. It begins with the Book of Genesis and is central to the creation narratives in the book's first two chapters in which we see the marital covenant formed between Adam and Eve within their covenant relationship with God (see Gen 2:21-24). This, in part leads St. John Paul II to discover marriage to be the primordial sacrament. The final book in the Christian Canon is the Book of Revelation. It culminates in the wedding feast of the Lamb (see Rev 19:7,9). This reveals that marriage and marital love is the institution by which God saves the world. Jesus' love for the Church enables Christian spouses love for one another to cooperate in His saving action. Scripture shows that marriage is a natural institution, authored by God with its proper meaning and its own laws. Marriage then is to be received by men (it is not his own creation), understood according to its given nature, and he must conform himself to it if it is to be authentic, fruitful and flourishing.

Complementary expressed love is the very essence of marriage. Marriage is a vocation that is written in man's nature as male-female, its proper ordering is essential to the good of the couple, to any children in the family, to the Church and to society. Man is created after the image and likeness of God, Who Is Love. Man is made for love, to give and to receive love. Marital love uniquely reflects Trinitarian love in its capacity to reflect the Trinitarian archetype in the fruitfulness of complementary, fruitful love. Complementarity means that men and woman are the same and at the same time, complementarily different. Both men and women possess a complete human nature, each is not "half" human. Therefore, they are equal in dignity before God. They are different in the way each possesses his human nature, and in the way their human gifts are primarily manifested in each sex. Men and woman are made for one another to "help" each other. They are called to become one flesh with one another in the marital covenant, revealing a complementary unity that is ordered to life-giving fruitfulness.

Original Sin causes disorder in this relationship. Due to the effects of original sin and to spiritual warfare, a spirit of domination of one spouse over the other can easily arise within the relationship. Therefore, the spouses must be constantly vigilant and master themselves to overcome this inclination. However, Jesus brings sanctifying grace into the Christian covenant of marriage, a grace necessary for the success and flourishing of the covenantal union. Jesus reveals that marriage in Him is indissoluble. He says that Moses on his own authority permitted divorce because of the hardness of the hearts of men, but Jesus shows that this is not God's law (see Mk. 10:2-12, Mt. 5:31-32; 19:3-11).

Jesus restores the original order of marriage, namely its irrevocability as the obligation of the covenant people because He brings the ability to live it by making it the very means of Christian spouses bestowing sacramental grace upon one another.

Generally, there are three things required for a valid Catholic marriage. They both must be of canonical age, men must be 17 years old, and women must be 15. Catholics must have the proper form, meaning they must be married by a deacon, priest, or bishop as the official witness, using the approved rite unless a previous dispensation is given by the bishop. The form is obligatory because every Sacrament is a liturgical event and because marriage is a state of life in the Church (it is an ecclesial order) it must be celebrated with approved witnesses. Finally, matrimonial consent is required of each partner for a valid marriage. Consent of each partner is the proper matter of the Sacrament. Each partner understands and freely consents to what the Church teaches about marriage and to this commitment to each other. Without this consent there is no marriage.

The requirements for their consent to be valid begins with ensuring that both partners are free to marry. This means that nothing constrains their ability to understand its meaning or their ability to freely commit themselves to it. They must not be compelled by other persons or circumstances to marry. The partners cannot be impeded by the natural law or by canon law. Each partner must understand that marriage is irrevocable, exclusive to the two of them, that they are committing to life-long fidelity to one another, and that they are committing to being open to having and raising children. Given this understanding of marriage, they commit to each other with the intention to live this covenantal commitment in their married lives.

In this fallen world, the matters of separation, civil divorce and annulments must be addressed. Since marriage is a Sacrament and an order in the Church, the Church has an interest in and responsibility to support the marriage. As such, canon law stipulates that the spouses may not separate or divorce without the permission of Church authority, unless there is immediate and grave danger to body or soul (see Can 1152-1153). While it may be unusual for a bishop to apply this aspect of canon law, the couple is still obligated to do all they can to remedy any problems in their marriage (e.g., getting spiritual guidance from their pastor, seeing a qualified marriage counselor, etc.). With respect to civil divorce, it is essential to understand that a valid marriage can never be dissolved except for the Pauline Privilege (see Can 1143). Therefore, while protection of the innocent spouse and/or children may permit the evil of a civil divorce, such a circumstance says nothing about its sacramental or natural validity.

If a civil divorce has been completed, both partners are still obligated to keeping their marriage vows. They may not date another person without violating their oaths of fidelity, irrevocability, and exclusivity. Such a violation is considered grave matter. If either partner believes that there was some defect rendering the marriage invalid from the start, he has the obligation to petition the Church to investigate the claim. If the appropriate marriage tribunal finds that the attempted marriage was in fact null, they will issue a decree of nullity. Only after each partner is in possession of this decree and has complied with all of its requirements (if any), is the partner free from the commitments previously made. An annulment (or more accurately, a decree of nullity) is a juridical finding that the marriage never existed and so the contracting parties are free to date and marry, but until such a decree is given, the marriage must be presumed to be valid.

There are obligations the couple must take care of in the case of what the Church calls mixed marriages and marriages that fall under the rubric of disparity of cult. Mixed marriages are between a Catholic and a non-Catholic Christian. This is no longer considered an impediment, but the couples must be helped to understand they risk experiencing the tragedy of Christian disunity even in their own home and have the obligation to face this risk together. The couple must receive *express permission* from the local bishop for the marriage to be licit. To receive this permission, the spouses must understand and agree to the essential ends of marriage, the Catholic spouse must agree to raise all children in the Catholic faith, and the non-Catholic spouse must acknowledge his spouse has this obligation. Disparity of cult refers to a marriage between a Catholic and a non-baptized person. The difficulties with disparity of cult can be even greater than with mixed marriages. Disparity of cult is an impediment to a valid marriage and so an *express dispensation* must be given by the local bishop for the marriage to be valid.

A valid marriage gives rise to a natural bond between the spouses, even if the bond is not sacramental, that is exclusive and irrevocable, obligating the couple to fidelity and openness to fertility. A sacramental marriage always exists in a valid marriage between a baptized man and baptized woman, which super-naturalizes the natural bond of marriage. A valid marriage cannot be sacramental if at least one partner is not baptized.

Conjugal love involves the totality of the person, including his intellect and will oriented especially toward spiritual communion and toward bodily unity which makes the two one-flesh, bringing them into a sort of personal unity of "one heart and soul." This obligates the two to inviolate fidelity in thought, word, and deed, guarding one's heart against temptations to even emotional infidelity. It also obligates the couple to the generosity of sharing this love with any children God might give them. Yet, children are not one's right but gifts. Acts that turn children into products by separating the procreative and unitive meaning of the marital act are always gravely immoral, such as surrogate motherhood, heterologous artificial insemination and fertilization, homologous artificial insemination and fertilization, or in vitro fertilization.

The Church is the family of God. The natural family provides the fabric of the members of the Church, so the early Church Fathers called the family the domestic church. Parents are the first and primary educators of their children, including in the faith. This education is a formation not simply in a formal classroom setting but in word and example throughout the lives of the children (of selfless love, fidelity, commitment, a life of the Sacraments and prayer, etc.). Parents cannot abandon this responsibility to others.

The Sacrament of Marriage is celebrated within the Mass for Catholics, and usually in the rite of Marriage outside of the Mass if one partner is not Catholic. It is always celebrated in a church. Penance is to be received prior to the marriage and Catholics should be Confirmed. The spouses are the ministers of the Sacrament of Marriage, to one another.

Sacramentals

Sacramentals are sacred signs, which bear resemblance to the Sacraments, except that they are instituted by the Church. They do not bestow grace, but rather prepare the recipient to be disposed to receive and cooperate with grace (especially through the Sacraments). They invoke the prayers of the entire Church for the particular intention. First among sacramentals are blessings of persons, meals, objects, places, etc. Blessings of consecration are those which consecrate persons or objects to God, or reserve objects and places to liturgical use. These blessings are of lasting importance. Exorcism is a sacramental blessing in which the Church publicly and authoritatively invokes in the name of Jesus, a person or object be protected against the power of the evil one.

NOTES

SESSION 14: THE MORAL LIFE & SOCIAL TEACHING

READING ASSIGNMENT

Pages 107-151: questions 357-433

STUDY QUESTIONS

Moral Life:

- Why is it that often when I get what I want, I am left unsatisfied? (CCCC qq: 358-400)
- How does Catholic moral teaching correspond with the rest of the faith? (CCCC q: 366)
- How can a moral life lead to a joyful life? (CCCC q: 361)

Catholic Social Teaching:

- How does the Church's social teaching correspond with its moral teaching? (CCCC qq: 401-414)
- Do I view social and political issues from the perspective of secular ideology rather than that of the Gospel? (CCCC qq: 402-404)
- How do the teachings on subsidiarity and solidarity go together? (CCCC qq: 403, 407)

NOTES:

Tutorial on the Moral Life

The moral life is irreplaceable for the path to communion. Because of concupiscence, it is a struggle against ourselves. Because of Satan, the path is also a spiritual battle. The more enslaved we are to our concupiscent desires, the more the moral life can seem to be contrary to our fulfillment. Contemporary society makes it even more difficult to see the beauty of Catholic moral teaching. It loudly proclaims the path to fulfillment is to satisfy our every desire indiscriminately, which is a path leading in precisely the opposite direction.

Freedom and Responsibility:

Human freedom is the power to use the intellect and will in order to act or not to act, which will result in some good or evil. Freedom is what makes man responsible for his voluntary acts and therefore makes him a moral subject.

Morality of an Act:

The morality of a human act depends upon three things: 1) the object chosen (which must always be authentically good), 2) the result intended, 3) the circumstances. The first two define the act as morally good or evil while the circumstances increase or decrease the act's praiseworthiness or its evil. The object is what anyone viewing the action from the outside sees (e.g., robbing a bank). Some "objects" are always morally evil and can never be justified such as the taking of innocent human life including abortion and euthanasia, fornication, lying, adultery, artificial birth control, same-sex acts, same-sex marriage, trafficking in the corpses of aborted children for any reason (such as for medical research), embryonic stem cell research, human cloning, etc. Such acts are called intrinsic evils.

The intention is the purpose known by the acting person (e.g., robbing the bank to buy critical medicine for one's child). A good intention cannot justify a morally evil action, nor can a good object excuse an evil intention. So both the object and intention must be good for an action to be good. For example, the desire to get needed medicine for one's child cannot make robbing the bank a morally good act. The circumstances increase or decrease the culpability for a bad act or they can increase or decrease the moral worthiness of a good act. In our example, the extreme stress from many fruitless efforts to pay for a child's critically needed medicine might decrease one's moral culpability making a gravely wrong act a venial sin, which wounds but does not rupture one's communion with God.

Conscience:

Conscience is a faculty comprised of a three-step process: 1) the awareness of absolute moral principles, 2) the application of these principles to concrete circumstances concerning an act about to be done or already performed, and 3) the judgment about the moral rightness or wrongness of the act. To be aware of absolute moral principles one must have a well formed, educated conscience. Properly forming a conscience is a lifelong task.

One must always choose in accord with one's conscience. To do otherwise is a sin. However, conscience is not an opinion, but a judgment based upon knowledge of absolute moral norms. One can make errors in judgment. If this occurs because of willful ignorance, one is responsible for the errors to the extent he was negligent. If one is invincibly ignorant, his culpability for any evil he commits due to this ignorance may be reduced or completely vitiated.

Sin is Rebellion Against Love:

As we have seen, sin is a turning away from God. It is choosing to be our own gods, without God. At its root, it is rebellion against God, Who is love. The moral life is nothing less than light for the path to communion. It reveals to us the acts which turn us inward. Morality is simply about choosing to love God and neighbor as were created to and about rejecting temptations that wound communion.

Self Mastery and Self Possession:

Communion is a relationship of total self-giving love. We fulfill ourselves by giving ourselves away. However, we cannot give to God and others what we do not first fully possess. The moral life is the school for self-mastery. We must master ourselves in order to say no to our selfish inclinations if we are to possess ourselves. The moral life reveals the traps that lead to isolation rather than communion, and it shows us how to avoid them. These traps can be identified in general through Christian moral teachings, especially those derived from the 10 Commandments (10 CCs). However, judging what is selfish versus selfless also requires applying moral norms to particular situations.

TUTORIAL ON THE VIRTUES

What is virtue? A virtue is a stable disposition within the person by which he can freely, joyfully and consistently choose the authentic good. Virtue gives one freedom to say no to evil and to say yes to authentic goods, unconstrained by the power of concupiscence that can limit his freedom. Virtue refers to the integrity of character which man in a fallen state must build in order to fulfill himself as a human person.

There are natural virtues and theological virtues, as well as infused virtues. What they have in common is that they are gained by developing habits that conform to human nature and its ultimate end. They are achieved through habitual acts appropriate to the development of each particular virtue (e.g., developing the virtue of courage requires the habitual choice to act rightly when fear or other difficulties would tempt one to act otherwise). The natural virtues are organized into four cardinal virtues. One virtue has to do with the intellect (prudence) and three involve the will (justice, temperance and fortitude). There are many other natural virtues that fall under each of these cardinal virtues, but we will focus on the four cardinal virtues in this chapter.

The theological virtues are related to the natural virtues. The natural virtues are rooted in the theological virtues of faith, hope and love, and they only grow to full maturity in concert with the maturation of the theological virtues. Faith, hope and love begin with God's invitation. One then responds through an act of the will, to surrender to God in faith (to trust in God and His promises, and to commit to Him), hope (faith projected into the future) and love (total self-gift). God then responds with the gift of Himself, by which our act of the will is super-naturalized and made redemptive. The supernatural virtues are deepened and perfected through continual acts of faith, hope and love by our cooperation with the grace of the Sacraments. The supernatural virtues have the fruit of super-naturalizing our efforts in building the natural virtues as well, leading us to the capacity to overcome enslavement to concupiscence and to gain increasing ability to choose, more freely and joyfully, the authentic good. It must be emphasized that concupiscence never goes away, but it becomes increasingly manageable through self-mastery perfected by grace.

The Four Cardinal Virtues

Prudence:

This is traditionally called the first of the virtues. It is first because prudence is always dictated by the truth of the created order and by the truth of the specific circumstances of a choice to be made. Prudence is the stable disposition of knowing how most effectively to attain some authentic good, ordered to the truth. Because every virtue is ordered by truth and by the authentic good, maturing all virtues is dependent upon prudence because it is required for knowing how to pursue them effectively.

Prudence is different from the other three Cardinal Virtues because they are good habits of the will, while prudence is a good habit in practical knowing. By practical we simply mean that it is knowing how to do something to bring the good about. Practical knowing is distinguished from speculative knowing. Speculative knowledge knows the truth and authentic goods by their essence, but it does not know how to achieve them. So, prudence begins with understanding reality, understanding what the authentic good is based upon the truth of reality/creation, and then seeing how to achieve the good in specific circumstances based upon this truth. For this reason, we can say that every sin is, in some manner, a violation against the virtue of prudence because sin is rebellion against the truth and the authentically good.

Justice:

This is the virtue by which one habitually gives God His due, which is everything. Giving God what is due to Him includes giving one's fellow man his due. Every person is due the freedom and opportunity, and assistance when necessary, for integral human flourishing. Integral human flourishing includes one's salvation, his perfection in love (holiness), and his intellectual, moral, emotional and bodily flourishing. Of course, there is a hierarchy among these human goods. This means that if a conflict arises among the human goods, the spiritual goods must take precedence, but we must also affirm that this does not make any of the lesser goods unimportant. Justice must always consider every good necessary for integral human flourishing.

Fortitude:

This is the stable disposition of being courageous in all circumstances. It means nothing other than the readiness to suffer harm and even death for the sake of the truth and for the sake of acting for authentic human goods. It ensures that we can overcome challenges to pursuing the good, and it helps us to be firm and consistent in facing evils in order to pursue integral human goods. As with all of the virtues, it is necessary to build it as a virtue because evil entered into the world with the fall of Adam and Eve. Cowardice and foolhardiness are fortitude's opposing vices, which have to be faced and overcome if we are to build fortitude. St. Thomas Aquinas says that fortitude serves to keep one from being deterred by fear of bodily harm from pursuing authentic human goods that one's reason has identified as necessary to be pursued. Therefore, the virtue of fortitude binds the will firmly to right reason in the face of the greatest evils.

Temperance:

This is the stable disposition of exercising self-discipline and moderation in the pursuit of created goods, particularly in their pursuit for the sake of the pleasure of the senses. Lack of temperance is often the key reason for our lack of virtue in general. In earlier chapters, we discussed the effects of the fall on the affects (i.e., the appetites and emotions), which we call concupiscence. We saw that they no longer respond harmoniously to the rational faculties as they were intended, and this is due to the loss of original grace. The Christian tradition of asceticism (especially fasting and abstinence), and the central importance of such acts in the admonitions of Christian spiritual masters demonstrate that the practice of self-mastery for temperance has long been recognized as essential to the Christian life.

Theological Virtues and Acts of Communion

There are three acts that are required for relationships of communion with God and with created persons: faith, hope and love. While similar, there is also a great difference in these acts in our relationship with God. Let's look at each in turn.

Faith:

Have you ever wondered why faith is necessary for salvation (see Mk 16:16)? Today's society considers skepticism, which is a rejection of faith, a virtue. Faith seems unreasonable to many today. If this is so, why would God require us to have faith? The answer to this requires understanding ourselves better.

Faith begins with trust; trust is eminently human. Trust is essential to live in a society. A quick audit of one's day will show that we trust automatically in almost everything we do. From food we eat, to what someone on the street tells us about himself, we trust unless we are given reason not to. We are made to have faith in others because we are made for relationships and so relationships are impossible without faith.

Faith has two aspects to it. The first is knowledge about who the person is. This knowledge is one of faith because it is mostly comprised of what the person has told us about himself, which we take on trust. When one is satisfied, he knows the other well enough, one may then commit to a relationship with him. This act of commitment is the second aspect of faith. This commitment is a sort of surrender of ourselves to the other person, which is different in quality based upon the type of relationship. So, faith is both a knowing based on trust and an act of the will committing to the person based upon this same knowledge.

Faith to this point is the same in our relationship with God and with human persons. Our knowledge of God is given through Divine Revelation by the Word of God, the Second Person of the Trinity. It is mediated down through time by human persons, some is written (the Bible) and some is oral (Apostolic Tradition).

We trust this knowledge because it comes from God through reliable witnesses. When one knows God sufficiently, one commits to Him in a way that surpasses every commitment to a human person. This commitment is a complete surrender of our entire selves to God. This "yes" is a human act of faith which commits us fully to God

172

and leads to our transformation. God responds with a gift of Himself. The fruit of this communion is participation in the divine nature (see 2 Pet 1:4), which is grace.

Grace elevates our natural faith to a supernatural virtue making it one of the three theological virtues. It is a virtue because it is maintained and strengthened by habit, by repetitively doing the same action. God ordinarily gives us this gift of Himself and His grace through the Sacraments.

Hope:

Hope is closely related to faith. One might describe hope as faith projected into the future. We commit to a person and our relationship with him not simply right now, but indefinitely. In some relationships, this commitment into the future includes certain specific commitments. For example, in marriage it is a commitment to lifetime fidelity and love regardless of what comes.

Hope in God is the commitment of our entire lives to Him and our trust in His promises of fidelity and love. These promises include His promise to help perfect us in loving Him and one another (which we call holiness). This promise extends beyond our earthly life to everlasting life if we persevere to the end of our lives in communion with Him. This commitment is made supernatural through the theological virtue of hope.

Love:

As necessary as faith and hope are for a relationship of communion with God and others, they count as nothing without love (see 1 Cor 13:1-3). Without works of love our faith is of no avail; it is no better than the belief of demons (Jas 2:17-19).

Love completes our total commitment to God and to others. If the relationship goes no further than faith, it is simply knowing the goodness of God and others, but it ends as a refusal to act in accordance with the requirements of true communion.

In the fourth session, we described the divine archetype of love as total self-giving. Man is made for the total, selfless giving of ourselves to God and to others. Of course, selfless giving takes different forms given the particular relationship.

Total selfless giving of ourselves in love to God means we follow our commitment of faith with action. Love for God means following His commands. His commands are summarized in the 10 commandments and the beatitudes. In general, this means avoiding all selfish actions and doing actions of selfless love for other persons.

Giving ourselves totally to God also means self-giving even to the point of giving up our mortal lives for His sake, if it should become necessary. Giving ourselves selflessly to human persons varies depending upon the relationship. More is required, for example, for our families than for those whom we don't know and who live at a great distance from us. However, what all selfless love has in common is that we "will" and "act" for the authentic good of the other person without regard to how such actions will benefit us.

The authentic good of others is that which leads them first to salvation and secondly to their integral natural good, body and soul. In other words, selfless love is not giving others whatever they want but what they require.

Love is, at its root, an act of the will. God commands us to love Him with our entire being and to love our neighbors as ourselves. He can only command us to do something we can do freely, something over which we have control. However, our experiences and social conditioning cause us to associate love with our feelings.

The feelings we associate with love, and there are a variety of them, are primarily the fruits of love. The feelings range from those that are primarily pleasure, to those that are natural joy, and finally to the joyful feelings of love that are super-naturalized. But it's a serious error to reduce love to feelings because love becomes fickle and not in our control.

In original innocence, with original grace, our feelings and our choosing naturally corresponded with one another. Today, our will and affects often don't correspond. We often mistake certain feelings for love that do not arise from authentic love. We will discuss this more in future sessions.

As mentioned in earlier, sex difference characterizes the structure of love between persons. Masculine love arises from the masculine soul's structure, which is visible in the masculine body. Masculine love is a love of first, initiation and then secondarily, active receptivity. Feminine love, again as one can see reflected in the female body, is the complement to this. Feminine love first actively receives love and then secondarily, initiates (or responds to) love in return. This complementary love is the prerequisite for spousal love, a fact that is confirmed in the bodily manifestation of this spiritual structure, that is, in the procreative capacity of the spouses' bodily complementarity.

TUTORIAL ON CATHOLIC SOCIAL TEACHING

Family and Society (CCC 2207-2233): Family is the foundation of society so flourishing societies require flourishing families, aided by society. A properly ordered society is possible when it recognizes God as the source of societal and family structure and authority. Parents are responsible for bearing and nurturing children in love, and forming them intellectually, morally, and spiritually. Children's duty is to obey their parents while in the home and honoring them after emancipation.

Authority in Civil Society (CCC 2234-2246): All authority in heaven and on earth comes from God (Rom. 13:1-2). Citizens have a duty to submit themselves to lawful authority, but to refuse obedience to unjust laws (e.g., abortion). While there is a distinction between the Church and political community, there isn't an absolute separation. The Church has the obligation and right to pass judgment on political, economic, and social matters. Classifying a matter as political or economic cannot exempt it from moral assessment.

Social Doctrine and the Church (CCC 2419-2463): The Church proposes several general social principles, which arise from the meaning of the human person who is an individual fulfilled only through relationships. Therefore, any social system that reduces social relationships to economic considerations is contrary the meaning of the human person and so immoral. Moreover, any theory making profit the norm and end of economic intercourse is morally inadmissible. Social systems subordinating authentic rights of individuals and/or groups to collective concerns (e.g., economic production) is contrary to human dignity. This includes collectivist ideologies which tend toward atheism and totalitarianism (e.g., communism and socialism) and radical individualist practices (e.g., a capitalism absolutizing laws of market forces over the good of persons).

Human Work (CCC 2426-2436): Work is a right and duty; it's the manner in which man co-creates with God. To deprive man from his right to participate in building up of society is an injustice, as is it for men to refuse to take part in this duty. Man loses his sense of dignity when deprived of participation in society through work. The state has a duty to ensure individuals' security, guarantee human rights, and preserve a just marketplace. Businesses have a duty to ensure positive economic and ecological fruits for the greater society, including paying a just wage.

Political principles (CCC 1883-85, 2209, 2437-42): *Subsidiarity* is a first principle stating that a community of a higher order should not interfere in a community of a lower order depriving it of its freedom. Social actions should take place at the lowest level possible. All state policies must be ordered to maximizing the ability of individuals social participation. *Solidarity* could be stated as "we are our brother's keepers." Political policies must be ordered to the common good, which includes the goods of the individuals. One cannot have subsidiarity without solidarity or vice versa; solidarity without subsidiarity is collectivism; subsidiarity without solidarity is radical individualism. They should be seen as co-principles, simultaneously political order.

Economic principles (CCC 2402-14): *Private property* states that everyone has a right to possessions so as to multiply the fruits of his labor, to provide for himself, his family and the common good. *Universal destination of goods* means God creates everything for the common good and so they must serve the common good. It isn't authentic private property without simultaneously obeying the principle of universal destination of goods. We are stewards over God's property; while we can't be deprived of it unjustly, if someone's life immediately depends upon use of our property available to them and it does not deprive us of our basic needs for life, we have an obligation to help them.

GRACE, VIRTUES AND THE GIFTS OF THE HOLY SPIRIT

Theology for Beginners by F.J. Sheed
Chapter 16

Sanctifying Grace – Free and undeserved gift of God which makes us partakers in the divine nature
Actual Grace – assistance given to all persons to respond to God's call

Fruit of the Holy Spirit – Galatians 5:22-23 & CCC 1832
Gifts of the Holy Spirit – Isaiah 11:1-2 & CCC 1831

Fruit of the Holy Spirit

Charity	**Joy**	**Peace**
Patience	**Kindness**	**Goodness**
Generosity	**Gentleness**	**Faithfulness**
Modesty	**Self-Control**	**Chastity**

GIFTS OF THE HOLY SPIRIT

WISDOM   **UNDERSTANDING**
COUNSEL   **FORTITUDE**
KNOWLEDGE   PIETY
FEAR OF THE LORD

Temperance   Fortitude
Prudence   Justice

LOVE

HOPE

FAITH

Theological Virtues: The Object is God (CCC 1812-1829)
    Faith: A gift from God in response to a human act of assent to Him and His revealed truth
    Hope: Our future oriented trust in God and in His promises of eternal life and the grace to attain it
    Love: Totally giving ourselves to God for His sake & selflessly acting for the good of our neighbor

Cardinal Virtues: The Object is Others and the World (CCC 1803-1809)
    Prudence: Sees the world as it is, orients us to discern the true good and how best to achieve it
    Justice: Gives to God and others what is due to them
    Temperance: Moderates the appetites so to use created goods for authentic human flourishing
    Fortitude: Gives us firmness in midst of difficulties to pursue the good and reject evil

SESSION 15: THE TEN COMMANDMENTS & THE BEATITUDES

READING ASSIGNMENT

Pages 126-151: questions 434-533

STUDY QUESTIONS

Ten Commandments:

- What in my life needs to change to better appreciate the gifts God has given me? (CCCC qq: 434-533)
- Do I have a spirit of docility toward God's commands? (CCCC qq: 434-533)
- How do I understand the relationship between the Ten Commandments and the Beatitudes? (CCCC qq: 434-533; 359-362)

Beatitudes:

- What do the Beatitudes mean for the way I live? (CCCC qq: 359-362)
- How do I need to look at my relationships differently given the demands of the Christian life? (CCCC qq: 455-465)

NOTES:

Tutorial on the Ten Commandments and the Beatitudes

10 CCs and the Hard Questions:

The Ten Commandments are the foundation of the moral life. They provide the moral norms which identify the risks we face because we live east of Eden. They are traditionally divided into two tablets. The first tablet is comprised of the first three commandments which show what is needed for a fulfilling relationship with God and the second tablet shows how we are to relate to others.

The 10 Commandments provide moral norms that are generally grave matter. For a sin to be mortal, the matter must be grave and there must be full knowledge and complete, free consent. Society today views many of these commandments as archaic opinions that modern people cannot reasonably hold. This is particularly true with the commandments associated with the sexual life. This makes these teachings "hard sayings" for many Catholics. However, it is especially these hard teachings that are most dangerous because breaking them leads us to selfishness, loss of self-mastery, and loss of communion while society says such actions lead to self-fulfillment.

For this reason, it is crucially important for us to fully understand the reason behind each of the Church's teaching on the moral issues we find hard and realize it makes much more sense to trust the Wisdom of Christ taught by His Church than the wisdom of a fallen world.

Beatitudes-Made for Heroic Love:

Everyone wishes to be a hero; it is written into our hearts. It is the desire to love heroically. Concupiscence and sin can bury this desire, but we are created to love by God, Love Himself. One can't flourish without giving and receiving love (see 1 Cor 13). Personal fulfillment comes through perfecting our ability to love God and to love others. Through the Cross, Jesus reveals that perfect love is totally giving oneself to God. But loving God is possible only by loving others; without love of neighbor we cannot have communion with God (1 Jn 4:20; Mt 5:43-48; Jas 2:14).

The Beatitudes are a ladder to perfect love (Mt 5:3-12). The first rung is the process of self-emptying, the prerequisite to total self-giving. Spiritual poverty prompts us to mourn our imperfect love. This promotes meekness, recognition that communion is a gift not a right. One then responds in desire for communion with God (i.e., righteousness), followed by acts of communion: showing mercy to others, turning oneself completely to God (purity of heart), and offering this gift of communion to others through evangelization (peacemaking). The final rung of the ladder is the gift of receiving the persecution Christ received, for His sake.

A PRIMER ON NATURAL FAMILY PLANNING

Natural Family Planning:
A Safe, Effective, and Moral Alternative to Contraception

Did you know?

1. Up until 1930, all Christians condemned artificial means of birth control. Today the Catholic Church stands alone in upholding this Christian truth.

2. In 1968, Pope Paul IV accurately predicted that condoning contraception would lead to increased marital infidelity, a lowering of morality, disrespect towards women, and a disregard for her physical and psychological health.

3. Those who use chemical birth control can increase their risk of breast cancer and other diseases.

According to a study published in the 8 January 1999 edition of the British Medical Journal women who used "the pill" experienced "significant increased mortality." For example, the risk of death from cervical cancer increased by approximately 200%, death from stroke increased 170% and circulatory diseases increased 120%.

Would You Like To Learn More?

Natural Family Planning Instruction:

San Antonio Diocesan NFP office: (210)734-2620 ext. 213

Couple To Couple League: (513)471-2000 or http://www.ccli.org/

World Organization Ovulation Method of Billings - http://www.woomb.org/index.shtml

Natural Family Planning Outreach (405)942-4084 or www.nfpoutreach.org

Effects of Contraception

One More Soul: 1-800-307-SOUL or http://www.omsoul.com/

Priests for Life 1-888-PFL-3448 http://www.priestsforlife.org/

Human Life International 540-622-5212 or http://www.hli.org/

Watch the bulletin and check in the back of both chapels for more information or contact Q & A with questions.

Top Ten Reasons to Use NFP

10. Because it works (see "Did you know" # 8,9).

9. Because it is natural, there are no dangerous side effects.

8. Because it will not destroy an unborn child (see "Did you know" #5).

7. Because marriage is a Sacrament and sexual relations bring about the renewal of the sacramental grace. God designed sex to be unitive and procreative and we must not separate the two. Contraception deliberately prevents two from becoming one (Gen2:24, Mk 10:8-9, Mt 19:5-6. Catechism of the Catholic Church 2363, 2366, 2370).

6. For your health and safety (see "Did you know" #3,4,6).

5. For the sake of your marriage (see "Did you know" #7).

4. Because of God's command to us, He said "Be fruitful and multiply." (Gn 1:28)

3. Because children are gifts from God (Gen. 17:16,20; 28:3; 29:32-35;Psalm 107:38; 127:5; 113:9 and too many more to mention). What would you do if someone treated your most precious gift as though it were a curse?

2. God has condemned it (God punished Onan for the "withdrawal method" as a capital crime in Gen. 38:7-10).

1. For the sake or your soul!

4. The younger you start the risk of breast cancer and death due to breast cancer.

A study published in the 1991 edition (vol. 15, issue 4) of South Sweden Cancer Detection and Prevention journal found that risk of death from breast cancer increased 820% for women starting on the pill prior to 20 years of age and 180% higher for those beginning on the pill between ages 20-25 years.

The same researchers, publishing in a 1989 issue (vol. 81, issue 12) of the Journal of the National Cancer Institute (of Sweden) showed that the risk of breast cancer is 200-480% higher in young women under age 20 who take the pill than for those who do not!

5. Every form of chemical birth control (the pill, Norplant, Depo-Provera) can cause early-term abortions.

6. *The Physician's Desk Reference* (and other medical sources) lists the following side effects of the pill: headaches, depression, decrease of sexual drive, abdominal cramps, weight gain, and more.

7. The divorce rate among couples who practice Natural Family Planning(NFP) is **LESS THAN** 5%. (This figure is according to a 1995 Couple to Couple League assessment).

8. NFP is a medically proven and highly effective method of achieving or postponing pregnancy by increasing a couple's fertility awareness.

9. Several medical studies have concluded that NFP is effective in avoiding pregnancy. It is just as effective as chemical birth control and more effective than condoms, diaphragms, and spermicides. We are **NOT** talking about the old Rhythm Method.

A US Department of Health Education and Welfare Study carried out in Los Angeles from 1976-78 found the NFP method from 96% (ovulation method) to 100% (Sympto-thermal) effective.

The 1978 Roetzer study found the average of the methods from 99-100% effective. This is compared to effectiveness rates for the pill of 90-96% as found in a 1988 Ohio State University Study, and 97% as listed in the 1998 Physian's Desk Reference.

10. The Catholic Church teaches and has always taught that each and every marriage must be open to life. (Catechism of the Catholic Church 2366, Didache*, Casti Connubii, Humanae Vitae 11, Familiaris Consortio**)

* *Didache* - Church manual and liturgical document written in the 1st Century that reflects the teaching of the apostles.
** *Encyclicals written by Popes Pius XI, Paul VI, and John Paul II respectively*

11. For just reasons (physical, psychological, emotional, financial) spouses may wish to space the births of their children. Birth regulation based on self-observation and the use of infertile periods respect the bodies of the spouses, encourage tenderness, and favors the education of an authentic freedom. (Catechism of the Catholic Church 2368, 2370)

12. We can trust the Catholic Church with this and all teachings dealing with faith and morals because.

The Church is the "pillar and foundation of truth (1 Tim. 3:15)

Because Jesus sent the Holy Spirit to guide it in all truth (John 16:13)

Because the Pope, along with the bishops as successors to the Apostles speak with the voice of the Holy Spirit (Acts 15:28)

PRECEPTS OF THE CHURCH

These five commandments are the laws that the Church gives to her faithful in order to provide the "indispensable minimum" required by Christians in terms of effort they must make in works of virtue and prayer if they are to remain on the path to heaven (see CCC 2041).

- **1st Precept** – "You shall attend Mass on Sundays and on holy days of obligation and rest from servile labor"

  This precept requires the faithful to sanctify the day commemorating the Resurrection of the Lord as well as the principle liturgical feasts honoring the mysteries of the Lord, the Blessed Virgin Mary, and the saints; in the first place, by participating in the Eucharistic celebration, in which the Christian community is gathered, and by resting from those works and activities which could impede such a sanctification of these days.

- **2nd Precept** – "You shall confess your sins at least once a year."

  This precept ensures preparation for the Eucharist by the reception of the sacrament of reconciliation, which continues Baptism's work of conversion and forgiveness.

- **3rd Precept** – "You shall receive the sacrament of the Eucharist at least during the Easter season."

  The precept guarantees as a minimum the reception of the Lord's Body and Blood in connection with the Paschal feasts, the origin and center of the Christian liturgy.

- **4th Precept** – "You shall observe the days of fasting and abstinence established by the Church."

  This precept keeps us observing the times of fasting, self-denial and penance which prepare us for the liturgical feasts and help us to acquire mastery over our instincts and freedom of heart. The days include fasting: all day on Ash Wednesday, Good Friday, and one hour before receiving Holy Communion (before Mass); as well as abstinence from meat on Ash Wednesday and on every Friday of the year (though outside of Lent some other food or penitential practice may be substituted).

- **5th Precept** – "You shall help to provide for the needs of the Church."

  The precept means that the faithful are obliged to assist with the spiritual and material needs of the Church, each according to his own ability.

(Taken from CCC 2042-43)

NOTES

SESSION 16: PRAYER & THE SPIRITUAL LIFE

READING ASSIGNMENT

Pages 159-191: questions 534-598

STUDY QUESTIONS

Prayer:

- Do I understand prayer as entering into a relationship of communion with God? (CCCC qq: 534-598)
- How much time would I spend in conversation with someone I really loved and what does this say about how I should consider my prayer life? (CCCC q: 575)
- How must I change my life in order to develop a fruitful, contemplative prayer life? (CCCC q: 571)

Spiritual Life:

- What do we mean by the spiritual life and what is its goal? (CCCC qq: 359, 361-365)
- How does my life of prayer help my spiritual life? (CCCC qq: 572-574)
- How high a priority do I place on my spiritual maturity? (CCCC q: 574)

NOTES:

TUTORIAL ON PRAYER AND THE SPIRITUAL LIFE

The spiritual life is not separate from the rest of our lives. In fact, it is affected by every choice we make. As such, we must always act in a way that conforms our hearts to Christ. In other words, we must always determine the most loving choice, choose to act in accordance with it, and thereby train our emotions to correspond to our wills.

The spiritual life is inseparable from the moral life, which trains the heart to make choosing authentic goods the easiest and most joyful option. But the spiritual life is also about knowing Christ more intimately so we can love Him more deeply. This is the basis for the Beatitudes, which reveal the fullness of the Law, Who is a person, Jesus Christ.

Prayer

What is Prayer?:

Prayer is a living, personal action of communion and love with God (see CCC 2558). It is an intimate encounter of love. If one can imagine what would occur in a relationship of intimacy in our human relationships without deep, intimate conversations with our loved one, we can see why a deep life of prayer is necessary for holiness. If the spiritual life is about working on deepening our relationship of love and intimacy with Jesus Christ, an intense prayer life cannot be dispensed with. One can rightly say that the intensity of one's prayer life is a direct reflection of the depth of one's spiritual life. There are five types of prayer, all of which are necessary for a deep life of prayer.

Types of Prayer:

BLESSING AND ADORATION (CCC 2626-2628): Blessing is the foundational expression of Christian prayer. When we bless God, we encounter Him in intimate communion. Indeed, when we pray, we are only responding to the Holy Spirit's initiative to pray. When we bless God, we are simply responding to God's invitation and in our response, He blesses us. That is, He gives us gifts (both spiritual and material), but most especially He gives us the gift of Himself, and we respond by blessing God through the Holy Spirit. In other words, we adore Him and return ourselves fully to Him.

Adoration is the first attitude we must have toward God. In adoration, we acknowledge God as our Creator. We recognize Him as the Source of all good; everything that exists and all the good things we have in our lives. When we adore God, we give Him homage and give ourselves to Him in total, self-giving love.

PRAYERS OF PETITION (CCC 2629-2633): These are the most common forms of prayer. They are prayers in which we ask God for our needs and desires. The first thing to realize is that petition expresses a relationship of dependence. We are completely dependent upon God for everything we have and are. We depend upon Him also for our salvation; it is not something we can earn or achieve by any other way but through surrender of ourselves to Him.

Our petitionary prayer should express our sorrow for our sinfulness but at the same time, it must be filled with hope in God's promises for He is trustworthy. We lament our sinfulness, but we also know that Christ won the war on the Cross. Our hope is in God's help to keep us from sin and through His grace, to bring us to Himself in eternity. This is not a pollyannaish optimism; it is a hope based upon God's fidelity and the price His Son paid to enable us to return to communion with Him. It is a hope that is grounded in the knowledge that our weaknesses are finite, but that God's strength is infinite. His strength enables us to overcome our weaknesses.

As with all prayer, the Holy Spirit inclines us toward all of our authentic petitions. Therefore, we must be docile in prayer, to the movement of the Holy Spirit. We must not enter into our petitions convinced that we know what is best and that we must pray hard to convince God. Rather, our prayers must be much more about God's informing us of His will and conforming us to that will.

The Catechism of the Catholic Church recommends a hierarchy to petitionary prayer. It should begin with asking God for forgiveness for our sins. This is a prerequisite for all authentic prayer. We then pray for the coming of His Kingdom and for the docility to cooperate with whatever is necessary to do our part to prepare the world for the Kingdom. In submitting ourselves, perhaps with the verbal expression "but thy will be done," our petitions are inclined to be authentic.

PRAYER OF INTERCESSION (CCC 2634-2636): When we intercede for the needs of others, we are following the example of our Master, Jesus Christ. We must pray for the integral human needs (spiritual and material) of our loved ones, our fellow Christians, our neighbors, even our enemies. We are moved to prayers of intercession by the initiative of the Holy Spirit, but when we consent to them, we mediate Christ's merciful love to others as His authentic disciples.

PRAYER OF THANKSGIVING (CCC 2637-2638): We have shown why the entire cosmos is Eucharistic. Prayers of thanksgiving are the heart of the Christian life. It is the prayer of the Church, especially in the Eucharist. By praying prayers of thanksgiving, we become more and more who we are, disciples of Christ and, as the Church, His spotless bride. There is no event, even a tragedy, for which we should not give thanks for His blessings, both seen and unseen.

PRAYER OF PRAISE (CCC 2639-2643): When we praise God, we do nothing more than express the truth. When we praise God, He does not get anything He does not already have. The one who benefits in prayers of praise is the one praising God. When we praise Him, we do so for His own sake and by this, we share in His joy through prayer that helps to purify our hearts.

Three Major Expressions of Prayer:

VOCAL PRAYER: Most prayer is vocal prayer, even when we pray quietly. Its importance is because of human nature's union of body and soul. Vocalization of our prayer unites the body and so our complete nature into one's interior prayer.

MEDITATION: Meditative prayer is a pilgrimage toward more intimate knowledge of God by engaging our intellects, our wills, our imagination, and our affects. The goal of meditative prayer is to interiorize within ourselves, with our entire being, the particular aspect of the faith upon which we are meditating (ultimately, this is God and His love). We can best do this by comparing our lives to the example of faith which we are considering and determining what is needed to close the gap. Everyone's prayer life must include a deep life of meditation.

CONTEMPLATIVE PRAYER: Contemplation is the simplest expression of prayer, which is intimate communion with God. When we contemplate, we fix our gaze on Jesus and surrender ourselves to Him in love. It is prayer beyond words, in which we can experience the deepest communion with Him in a way that makes our encounter with Him in the Eucharist more fruitful. It is also the most difficult expression of prayer for those who live frenetic lives and who find it almost torture to sit in silence for more than a few moments. However, it is in the silence of our hearts that we most clearly hear Jesus Christ and are enabled to give ourselves fully to Him.

The Battle for Prayer:

Prayer is a battle against our fallen nature and against Satan's temptations. Satan will use our wounds against us to tempt us away from this form of communion with God. Prayer is not a human invention. It is God's gift to us but it also demands our active cooperation. The first step in prayer is to assume the attitude of humility, recognizing Who God is and who we are. When we recall our complete dependence upon Him, we are prepared to encounter God in the proper disposition of thanksgiving.

Prayer requires our active attention. We need to be aware of and vigilant over our thoughts. We must immediately dismiss any distractions, including the temptation to ponder the source of the previous distraction. This itself is a demonic temptation to keep us distracted. Prayer requires perseverance. We have to persevere through periods of dryness. Remember we do not pray for the way it makes us feel. We do not pray to "get" something out of it. These are fruits of prayer, not its essence.

Prayer is communion with God; prayer is an end in which we give ourselves to Him. We need to surrender ourselves to God in childlike trust. It is not we who will bring about the efficacy of our prayer lives. While we must do our part to possess ourselves so we have ourselves to give totally to God, it is the Holy Spirit Who brings about the fruitfulness. If we keep our eyes on the Cross, we are less likely to be dissuaded from prayer by these common pitfalls.

NOTES

SESSION 17: THE LAST THINGS – DEATH, JUDGMENT, HEAVEN & HELL

READING ASSIGNMENT

Pages 38-41: questions 125-135; pages 56-59: questions 202-217

STUDY QUESTIONS

Death:

- How much time do I spend considering my death and what this means for the way I live? (CCCC qq: 205-206)

Judgment:

- Do I daily consider my particular judgment day when making my decisions and setting my life's priorities? (CCCC q: 208)

Heaven:

- Do I consider God's invitation to spend eternity in ecstasy with Him? (CCCC q: 209)
- Do I consider what an eternity in a redeemed body means for the dignity and holiness of the body? (CCCC q. 202)

Hell:

- Do I consider what eternity would be like separated from Him for Whom I have been created as well as separated from everyone else; that is, spending my eternity all alone, turned in upon myself? (CCCC q: 212)

NOTES:

TUTORIAL ON THE LAST THINGS:

Eschaton: Eschaton is a Greek work meaning "last," which the Christian tradition uses to indicate the end of times, when Jesus returns again in glory to judge the living and the dead. The traditional Last Things are death, judgment, heaven and hell.

Death: Death is the separation of the soul from the body; the body decays and the soul meets God in the Particular Judgment awaiting the Final Judgment when the body will undergo Resurrection and be rejoined with the soul— "those who have done good to the resurrection of the life, and those who have done evil to the resurrection of judgment." (see Jn 5:29; CCC 997, 998, 1005).

Death was not originally part of God's plan but came into the world due to sin; Jesus has conquered death and we, provided we die with Him, shall live with Him (CCC 1008-1009). Death marks the end of our journey on earth; the last opportunity to work out our salvation according to God's divine plan, and to decide our ultimate destiny by accepting or rejecting His saving grace. There will be no second chance, there is no return to earth, no reincarnation.

Judgment:

Particular Judgment At the moment of our death, we shall be immediately judged and we will be justly rewarded for our faith and works of love. We shall go to everlasting life in heaven (immediately or through purification), or immediately to everlasting damnation (Mt 7:1-2).

Purgatory: All who die in a state of grace but are still imperfectly purified will undergo purification. The Church calls this final purification of the elect Purgatory, which is entirely different than the punishment of the damned. Purification removes the stains of forgiven mortal sins (for which reparations have not yet been fully made) or unforgiven venial sins. Scripture speaks of Purgatory as a cleansing fire (see 1 Cor 3:10-15; 1 Pt 1:7; 1 Cor 6:9-10).

Final Judgment: The Resurrection of the dead (both just and unjust) precedes the final judgment. Every thought, word and deed will be laid bare before us, even to its furthest consequence. The last judgment will come with the Parousia, when Christ returns again in glory. Only the Father knows the hour; only He determines the moment. Then we shall know the entire meaning of all creation. All the just will be joined in heaven where the elect will be given glorified bodies. The damned will be condemned to everlasting torment in hell. At the end of time, the kingdom of God will come into its fullness; the universe itself will be renewed. The visible universe will be transformed, restored to its original state to be at the service of the just (CCC 1046). The Final Judgment is depicted in Mt 25:31-46.

Resurrection of the Body: Restoration of creation to the communion for which God created it will begin with the body's resurrection. Those in communion with God will resurrect to everlasting life by receiving a glorified body. A glorified body is in complete harmony with the soul, and the body-soul is perfectly permeated with the life of the Holy Spirit; man will finally be fully alive. Those who have rejected communion will receive a body of judgment; a body that is in complete conflict with the soul; a conflict that will be a source of unspeakable, everlasting pain.

Reconciliation of All Things in Christ: After the Resurrection, Christ will return with all His angels to judge both the living and the dead. He will come in glory in which there will be no doubt He has come for the final judgment. The just who have chosen communion by loving Christ in serving the least of their brothers will go to eternal life. Purgatory will now be empty and abolished. Those who have rejected love by refusing to help the least of their brothers will go to everlasting damnation (see Mt. 25:31-46). The final judgment will reveal to each person all the good he did or failed to do and its furthest implication for bringing others to communion with God. Everything will be brought under the authority of one Head, Jesus Christ. He will return all things, over which He rules, to His Father.

Heaven: Heaven is also referred to as the beatific vision because then we shall see Him face to face (1 Jn 3:2). This perfect life with the Most Holy Trinity, with the Virgin Mary, the angels and blessed is called Heaven. Heaven is the blessed community of all who are perfectly incorporated into Christ (1 Cor 2:9).

New Heavens and New Earth: At the end of time, not only persons who are saved but the entire cosmos will be restored to full communion with God. Creation will be fully interpenetrated by the life of the Holy Spirit. This, Scripture calls "a new heavens and a new earth." This renewed cosmos will be fully at the service of those in communion with God, forming a great cosmic communion in Christ. The communion for which creation now groans in travail, will finally be restored.

Hell: If we die in mortal sin without repenting and accepting God's merciful love, we will spend eternity separated from Him for Whom we were made. This is by our own free choice. This state of permanent separation from God is called Hell. The Church affirms the existence of Hell, its eternity, and its eternal fire of punishment; the chief punishment is separation from God, in whom alone man can possess the life and happiness for which he was created (Mt 7:13-14; 25:46).

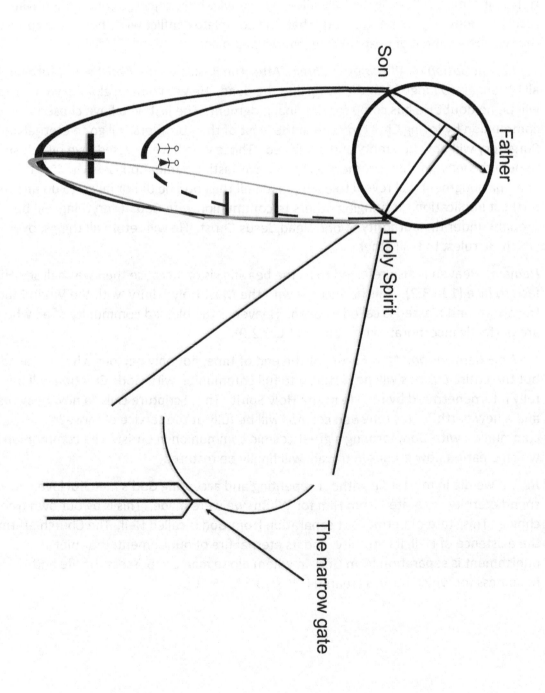

Notes

NOTES

APPENDIX 1: KNOWING WHEN YOU ARE READY

It is not always easy to recognize when one is ready to come into full communion with the Catholic Church. There are often many motivating reasons, such as wanting to share the faith with one's family or future spouse, to make others happy, because one is dissatisfied with one's own tradition, etc. Whatever the motivation, one can be sure to being ready when able to answer "yes" to the following questions:

- Have I made the decision to surrender my entire life to Jesus Christ?
  - o Am I prepared to let Him guide every aspect of my personal life, family and work?
  - o Since surrendering, have I started to eliminate sinful habits from my life?
  - o Have I begun to share my new-found faith with others?
- Do I believe the fundamental dogmas of the faith, such as:
  - o Do I believe that God is one perfect nature in Three Persons—Father, Son and Holy Spirit?
  - o Do I believe that Jesus Christ is true God and true Man?
  - o Do I believe that Jesus Christ is the only way to salvation through Baptism in faith?
  - o Do I believe the meaning and necessity of the seven Sacraments, especially that the Mass is the true Sacrifice of the Cross made present on the altar?
  - o Do I believe that Jesus Christ is present, Body, Blood, Soul and Divinity in the Eucharist?
- Do I believe that Jesus Christ established one Church on St. Peter and His successors the popes, and that this is the Catholic Church?
- Do I believe that one is in full communion with Jesus Christ when in full communion with the Pope, the keeper of the keys?
- Do I trust that the Holy Spirit faithfully guides the Church in truth, so that I can obediently accept even those of her teachings I may not fully understand?
- Do I accept the social and moral teachings of the Catholic Church, because they are Jesus' teachings, and that while I may not fully know or understand all her teachings, it is my obligation to educate myself as a member of the Church and society on such pressing social issues as abortion, homosexuality, laws governing marriage, and a preferential love of the poor?
- Am I willing to accept and follow all of the disciplinary requirements of the Church? These include days of fasting and prayer, holy days of obligation, my duty to support my church, and other practical teachings of the Church that are necessary for her institutional life.

Entering the Church is the beginning, not the end of your journey. Ahead of you is a lifetime of learning what it means to be a true disciple of Christ. There may still come times of struggle, boredom or doubt, but as long as you persevere with a spirit of docility and openness to truth, your journey will be fruitful.

"I have fought the good fight, I have finished the race, I have kept the faith. Henceforth there is laid up for me the crown of righteousness, which the Lord, the righteous judge, will award to me on that Day, and not only to me but also to all who have loved his appearing." 2 Tim 4:8

APPENDIX 2: CATHOLIC READING LIST

The Catholic Faith
Catechism of the Catholic Church, Part 1
Compendium of the Catechism of the Catholic Church
The Faith of the Early Fathers, William A. Jurgens
Hail, Holy Queen – Scott Hahn
Theology for Beginners, Frank Sheed
Theology and Sanity, Frank Sheed
To Know Christ Jesus, Frank Sheed
The Catholic Faith Video Series, Mother of the Americas Institute
(www.mainstitute.org/resources)

The Liturgy and the Sacraments
The Lamb's Supper, Scott Hahn
Catechism of the Catholic Church, Part 2
Jesus and the Jewish Roots of the Eucharist, Brandt Pitre
Liturgy 101: Sacraments and Sacramentals, Daniel G. Van Slyke
The Spirit of the Liturgy, Joseph Ratzinger
The Glory of Service, Aidan Nichols, OP

Marriage and Family Life
Sex and the Marriage Covenant, John Kippley
Love and Responsibility, Karol Wojtyła
Covenant of Love, Richard M. Hogan & John M. LeVoir
Male and Female He Created Them, Jorge Cardinal, Medina Estevez
Called to Love, Carl Anderson, Jose Granados

Church History
Triumph, H.W. Crocker, Jr
The Catholic Church Through the Ages, John Vidmar, OP
A Summary of Catholic History (2 volumes), Newman Eberhardt
History of the Church of Christ, Henri Daniel-Rops
A Popular History of the Church, Philip Hughes

The Moral Life
Catechism of the Catholic Church, Part 3
Our Moral Life in Christ, Aurelio Fernandez & James Socias

Morality: The Catholic View, Servais Pinckaers, OP
Vices & Virtues, Alejandro Ortega Trillo

Apologetics
Radio Replies, Frs. Rumble and Carty (3 Vols)
Catholicism and Fundamentalism, Karl Keating
Rome Sweet Home, Scott and Kimberly Hahn
Orthodoxy, G.K. Chesterton
Surprised by Truth (series), Patrick Madrid
Catholic for a Reason (series), Scott Hahn and Leon J. Suprenant Jr.
Search and Rescue, Patrick Madrid

Scripture Study
A Father Who Keeps His Promises, Scott Hahn
Navarre Bible Series, Navarre University
Ignatius Catholic Study Bible (series), Curtis Mitch & Scott Hahn
A Catholic Commentary on Holy Scripture
A New Catholic Commentary on Holy Scripture
Companion to Scripture Studies, John Steinmueller

The Spiritual Life
Catechism of the Catholic Church, Part 4
Forty Weeks, William J. Watson, SJ
Discerning the Will of God, Timothy M. Gallagher, OMV
The Examen Prayer, T. M. Gallagher
The Discernment of Spirits, T. M. Gallagher
Story of a Soul, St. Therese of Lisieux
The Three Conversions of the Spiritual Life, Reginald Garrigou-Lagrange, OP
Confessions, St. Augustine
Fire Within, Thomas Dubay, SM
Dark Night of the Soul, St. John of the Cross
Interior Castles, St. Teresa of Avila
Introduction to the Devout Life, St. Francis de Sales
The Virtues, Benedict XVI
Resisting the Devil: A Catholic Perspective on Deliverance, Neal Lozano

Made in the USA
Coppell, TX
13 December 2023